D0128777

Instant Immersion™

Italian

developed by Mary March, M.A.

written by Kristin Salerno, Ed.M.

TOPICS

ENTERTAINMENT®

© 2003 Topics Entertainment, Inc.

1600 S.W. 43rd Street, Renton, WA 98055 U.S.A.

www.topics-ent.com

All rights reserved. No part of this book may be reproduced or transmitted in any form or by any means, electronic or mechanical, including photocopying without permission in writing from the Publisher.

Instant Immersion™

developed by Mary March, M.A.
written by Kristin Salerno, Ed.M.

ISBN 1-59150-311-6

Edited by Giulia Guarnieri
Creative Director: Tricia Vander Leest
Illustrations by Elizabeth Haidle
Art Director: Paul Haidle
Design by Paul Haidle
Maps by Lonely Planet®

Printed on 100% recycled paper. Printed in the U.S.A.

TABLE OF CONTENTS

INTRODUCTION

Benvenuto (welcome) to *Instant Immersion Italian*™! An understanding of other cultures is critical to becoming part of a larger global community. Knowing how to communicate in other languages is one way to facilitate this process. You have chosen a truly global language to learn. There are diverse Italian cultures in Europe, Canada, the United States, and South America, having a worldwide influence on cuisine, fashion, dance, theatre, architecture, and arts. Italian is also the official working language of many international organizations.

Now let's get down to learning some Italian. Did you know that close to half of all English vocabulary has roots in the Italian language? This means you already know the meaning of many Italian words that look very much like their English equivalents: *musica, banana, nazionalità, bicicletta, ospedale,* and *lettera* are only a few. You just have to learn the pronunciation. (And you will see that learning Italian pronunciation is not as difficult as you might think!)

This book will help you learn the basics of communicating in Italian in a way that will be fun and easy for you. We include many popular phrases and expressions and show you how these are used in real life through example conversations and stories. Our book also provides an easy pronunciation system that will give you the confidence you need to speak Italian. A wide range of interesting and valuable topics give you a firm grounding in the language, including how to order food like a local, how to travel comfortably within the country, even what to do when things go 'wrong'. *Buona fortuna!*

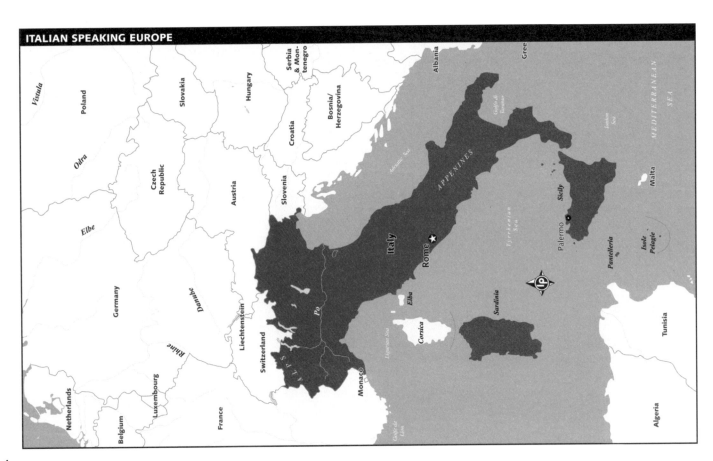

PRONUNCIATION GUIDE

The following is a key of phonetic pronunciation as you will find in the coming chapters. Note the example of the Italian word, then the written pronunciation. Refer to this key when you cannot remember what the pronunciation is supposed to reveal. Articulation of vowels and consonants are clarified as they pertain to American English.

VOWELS:

A	–	*ah*	casa	*(kahsah)*
E	–	*eh*	prego	*(prehgoh)*
I	–	*ee*	panini	*(pahneenee)*
O	–	*oh*	bello	*(behlloh)*
U	–	*oo*	cugina	*(koojeenah)*

CONSONANTS:

B	–	*b*	bene	*(behneh)*
C	–	*k*	casa	*(kahsah)*
CI/E	–	*ch*	c'è	*(cheh)*
CH	–	*k*	chianti	*(keeahntee)*
D	–	*d*	donna	*(dohnnah)*
F	–	*f*	fratello	*(frahtehlloh)*
G	–	*g*	gatto	*(gahttoh)*
GI/E	–	*j*	giorno	*(johrnoh)*
GN	–	*ny*	gnocchi	*(nyohkee)*
H	–	*( )*	**will not appear by itself; rather only with c (see above)
L	–	*l*	lunedì	*(loonehdee)*
M	–	*m*	martedì	*(mahrtehdee)*
N	–	*n*	natale	*(nahtahleh)*
P	–	*p*	padre	*(pahdreh)*
Q	–	*k*	acqua	*(ahkooah)*
R	–	*r*	rosso	*(rohssoh)*
S+vowel		*z*	spesa	*(spehzah)*
SS	–	*s*	spesso	*(spehssoh)*
T	–	*t*	sabato	*(sahbahtoh)*
V	–	*v*	Vincenzo	*(veenchehntsoh)*
Z	–	*ts*	zucca	*(tsookah)*

DOUBLE CONSONANTS AND VOWELS:

Anytime you see two consonants or vowels next to each other, the pronunciation will call for two as well in order to remind you to elongate the sound:

giallo	–	*jahlloh*
zii	–	*dzee-ee*

Instant Immersion™ Italian has 16 chapters. You can work through the book chapter by chapter or skip around to the topics that most interest you. Study the expressions and vocabulary before reading the dialog or story. Say them out loud to practice your pronunciation. Read through the dialog or story as many times as you need for understanding. Then read it out loud. Check your answers to the exercises in the Answer Key in the back of the book. Finally, get in an Italian mood! Cook a delicious bowl of pasta, drink a glass of Chianti, play some music by Ligabue or Andrea Bocelli, buy a Sicilian granita, speak English with an Italian accent, whatever it takes.... But have fun learning Italian!

CHAPTER 1

(boo-oh johrnoh)
Buon giorno!
Good morning!

The Italian *alfabeto* is a phonetic and musical group of letters and sounds representing the Italian language. As you try these letters and sounds, allow your mouth, lips, and voice to exaggerate the pronunciation. The more you enunciate, the more natural your Italian will sound. Remember, Italians are experts at communicating.

(nohn mee eempohrtah)
Non mi importa.
No big deal./It doesn't matter.

(fah loh stehssoh)
Fa lo stesso.
It's the same for me./It's all the same to me.

(ahndeeahmoh)
Andiamo.
Let's go.

VOCABULARY

(loo-ee)
lui
he

(loo-ohmoh)
l'uomo
man

(lah mahtteenah)
la mattina
morning

(leh-ee)
lei
she

(lah dohnnah)
la donna
woman

(pahrlahreh)
parlare
to speak

(boo-ohn johrnoh)
Buon giorno
Good morning

(kohmeh stah-ee)
Come stai (tu)?
How are you?

(ee-oh stoh behneh)
Io sto bene
I'm fine

(too)
tu
you

(vohlehreh)
volere
want

(eel pahneh)
il pane tostato
toast

(fahreh)
fare
to make/to do

(ahndahreh)
andare
to go

(manjahreh)
mangiare
to eat

(lah chehnah)
la cena
dinner

(eel prahntsoh)
il pranzo
lunch

(lah kohlahtsee-ohneh)
la colazione
breakfast

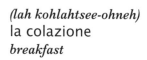

7

DIALOG

E' mattina. Una donna (Annalisa) e un uomo (Paolo) parlano.

Annalisa: "Buon giorno Paolo" "Come stai?"

Paolo: "Buon giorno, Annalisa. Io sto bene, e tu?

(voo-ohee)
Annalisa: "Io sto bene. Dove vuoi fare colazione?"

(pohtrehmmoh)
Paolo: "Fa lo stesso. Potremmo andare a mangiare

(ahlbehrgoh)
del pane tostato a un caffè, in albergo."

(ahnkee-oh)
Annalisa: Anch'io. Allora, Andiamo!"
Me too

PRACTICE

colazione	cena	volere	avere (take)
pranzo	dove	tu	andare

Fill in the blanks using the words in the box below.

1. _____ vuoi fare _____ ? 8 p.m.

2. Dove _____ _____ fare _____ ? 12 noon

3. Dove vuoi _____ _____ _____ ? 8 a.m.

4. _____ vuoi mangiare?

MATCHING

Match the sentence with the picture.

_____ 1. Un uomo e una donna parlano.

_____ 2. Anch'io. Allora andiamo!

_____ 3. Fa lo stesso.

_____ 4. E' mattina.

_____ 5. Dove vuoi fare colazione?

_____ 6. Io vorrei mangiare?

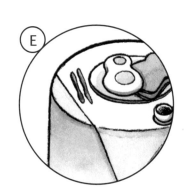

FOCUS

SUBJECT PRONOUNS

	Singular			Plural	
I	io	*(ee-oh)*	we	noi	*(noh-ee)*
you	tu/Lei	*(informal/formal) (too/Leh-ee)*	you	voi	*(voh-ee)*
he	lui	*(loo-ee)*	they	(m) loro	*(lohroh)*
she	lei	*(leh-ee)*	they	(f) loro	*(lohroh)*
it	lui/lei	*(loo-ee/leh-ee) (almost always, nothing is used but the verb conjugation)*			

VERB CONJUGATIONS

(mahnjahreh)
mangiare
to eat

Io mangio un po'.
a little

Noi mangiamo molto.
a lot

Tu mangi la carne.
meat

(pahstah)
Voi (plural) mangiate la pasta.
pasta

(mahkeenah)
Lei mangia in macchina.
car

(spee-ahjah)
Loro mangiano sulla spiaggia.
beach

Lui mangia sulla spiaggia.
beach

(lehttoh)
Loro mangiano a letto.

```
                        M A N G I A R E

    io mangio              (ee-oh mahnjoh)                      I eat
    tu mangi               (too mahnjee)                        you eat
    lui/lei/Lei mangia     (loo-ee/leh-ee/Leh-ee mahnjah)      he/she/you (formal) eat
    noi mangiamo           (noh-ee mahnjahmoh)                  we eat
    voi mangiate           (voh-ee mahnjahteh)                  you (plural) eat
    loro/Loro mangiano     (lohroh mahnjahnoh)                  they eat
```

```
                         A V E R E
                        (ahvehreh)
                         to have

    io ho              (ee-oh oh)              I have
    tu hai             (too ah-ee)             you have
    lui/lei/Lei ha     (loo-ee/leh-ee ah)      he, she has
    noi abbiamo        (noh-ee ahbeeahmoh)     we have
    voi avete          (voh-ee ahvehteh)       you have
    loro hanno         (lohroh ahnnoh)         they have
```

Note: Notice that many expressions in Italian with avere + noun are expressed in English
        with be + adjective: I am thirsty   *Io ho sete.*   (I have thirst.)

        Notice also that the Italian use avere to state their age: *Io ho dieci anni*   ("I have
        10 years old" rather than "I am 10 years old." However... *Io sono stanco* (I am tired.)

Here are some common expressions
with the verb avere – "to have":

(ee-oh oh pow-oorah)
Io ho paura.
I'm afraid.

(ee-oh oh sohnnoh)   *(ee-oh oh beezohnyo dee...)*
Io ho sonno.   Io ho bisogno di...
I'm sleepy.   *I need...*

(voh-ee ahvehteh rahjohneh)   *(voh-ee ahvehteh sehteh)*   *(too ah-ee frehttah)*
Voi avete ragione.   Voi avete sete.   Tu hai fretta.
You're right.   *You're thirsty.*   *You're in a hurry.*

CHAPTER 2

(oh fahmeh)
Ho fame!
I'm hungry!

Reading in *italiano* will help you learn how to understand the language. It is an easy, effective way to increase your vocabulary and knowledge of grammatical structures. Practice saying the idioms and vocabulary words. Study the meaning of each. Then read the story silently, trying to understand it. Read the story again out loud, focusing on the pronunciation of the words.

(keh fohrtoonah)
Che fortuna!
What luck!

(oh fahmeh)
Ho fame!
I'm hungry!

VOCABULARY

(ehntrah)
entra
enter

(pahrteh)
parte
leave

(fehleecheh)
felice
happy

(treesteh)
triste
sad

(lyee ahmeechee)
le amiche
female friends

(eel fohrmahjoh)
il formaggio
cheese

(dah)
da
give

NUMBERS

If you want to understand a room number, tell someone your phone number, or understand how much something is you are considering buying, you need numbers. Try to memorize the numbers 0–10 now. (Practice counting throughout the day!) More numbers will be introduced in later chapters.

0	1	2	3	4	5
(dsehroh)	*(oonoh)*	*(doo-eh)*	*(treh)*	*(koo-ahttroh)*	*(cheenkwehee)*
zero	uno	due	tre	quattro	cinque

6	7	8	9	10
(seh-ee)	*(sehtteh)*	*(ohttoh)*	*(nohveh)*	*(dee-ehchee)*
sei	sette	otto	nove	dieci

PRACTICE

Write the answers to these simple arithmetic problems in words.

1. tre più uno = _____

2. sei più quattro = _____

3. due più tre = _____

4. otto meno cinque = _____

5. nove meno otto = _____

6. dieci meno tre = _____

7. quattro per due = _____

8. tre per tre = _____

STORY

(ahmeekah)   *(reestohrahnteh)*
Anna e la sua amica Giulia sono al ristorante.

(pahneenoh)
Anna mangia un panino al formaggio.

(Jahkohmoh)
Giulia prende due panini al formaggio.

Giacomo entra nel ristorante.
enters

(prehzehntah)
Anna presenta Giulia a Giacomo.

(pee-ahchehreh dee kohnohshehrtee)
Giacomo a Giulia: "Piacere di conoscerti Giulia",

(kee-ehdeh)
dice Giacomo. Poi Anna chiede a

Giacomo se lui ha fame. "Sì, ho fame!" dice lui.

Giulia dà a Giacomo un panino.

(reespohndeh)
"Che fortuna!" risponde Giacomo.

Lui è molto felice.

PRACTICE

The statements below are all false. Change each one to make it true.

1. Anna e la sua amica mangiano in una macchina.

   _____

2. Giulia prende tre panini. _____

3. Giacomo esce dal ristorante. _____

   (ehsheh)

   exits

4. Giacomo è triste. _____

VERB FOCUS

(ehssehreh)
essere
to be

Noi siamo felici.
We are happy.

Tu sei felice.
(familiar)
You are happy.

Lei è felice.
She is happy.

Loro sono felici.
They are happy.

Io sono triste.
I am sad.

Voi siete tristi.
(plural)
You are sad.

Lui è triste.
He is sad.

Here are some useful sentences with the verb "be":

(dahkkohrdoh)
Io sono d'accordo.
I agree.

(mahnjahndoh)
Loro stanno mangiando.
They are eating.

(een reetahrdoh)
Noi siamo in ritardo.
We are late.

(dohttohrehssah)
Lei è la mia dottoressa.
She is my doctor.

(vahleejah)
La valigia nera è mia.
The black suitcase is mine.

CHAPTER 3

(skoozee)
Scusi!
Excuse me or Sorry!

If you are traveling to a foreign country, there will be many opportunities for you to start a conversation with native speakers of the language. Don't be shy! Of course some people will be in a hurry or won't want to talk to you. However, many people will be interested to meet someone traveling in their country. You'll want to learn some basic questions and appropriate responses as well as some useful expressions.

(ee-oh oh sehteh)
Io ho sete.
I am thirsty.

(ee-oh sohnoh stahnkoh)
Io sono stanco.
I am tired.

Non importa.
It doesn't matter.
OR It's not serious.

VOCABULARY

(see)
sì
yes

(dah)
da
from

(dohveh)
dove
where

(vehneereh)
venire
to come

(lah feelyah)
la figlia
daughter

(pahrlahreh)
parlare
to speak

(ehkkoh)
ecco
here (is/are)

(e'eel mee-oh nohmeh eh)
il mio nome
my name is

(oon poh)
un po'
a little

(eel feelyoh)
il figlio
son

USEFUL EXPRESSIONS

Here are some ways to say yes and no:

(see)
Sì!
Yes!

(noh)
No!
No!

(chehrtoh)
Certo!
Certainly!

(seekoorahmehnteh noh)
Sicuramente no!
Of course not!

(dee seekooroh)
Di sicuro!
Sure! Of course!

(ahl kohntrahreeoh)
Al contrario!
On the contrary!

Sometimes bumping into people by accident can lead to introductions and even friendships. Read what Daniele and Silvia have to say to each other after they bump into each other in a doorway.

(lah dohnnah)
Silvia: la donna
the woman

(eel rahgahtsoh)
Davide: il ragazzo
the boy

(lah rahgahtsah)
Sofia: la ragazza
the girl

(loo-ohmoh)
Daniele: l'uomo
the man

1 | **Daniele:** Scusi!

Silvia: No importa.

2 | *(sehee ahmehreekahnah)*
Daniele: Sei americana?

Silvia: Sì! Di dove sei tu?

3 | **Daniele:** Io sono di Seattle nello stato di Washington.

Il mio nome e' Daniele Donato. E tu? Qual e' il tuo nome?

4 | **Silvia:** Il mio nome è Silvia Simonetta.

(peeahchehreh dee cohnohshehrtee)
Piacere di conoscerti.

(nice to meet you)
Daniele: Piacere di conoscerti.

5 | *(feelyah)*
Silvia: Ecco mia figlia, Sofia.
daughter

Daniele: Ciao, Sofia. Quanti anni hai (tu)?

6 | **Sofia:** Ho otto anni.

(feelyoh)
Daniele: Ecco mio figlio, Davide.
son
Lui parla un po' d'italiano.

Sofia: Ciao, Davide.
Quanti anni hai (tu)?

Davide: Io ho cinque anni.
Ho fame e ho sete. Sono stanco.

PRACTICE

Study the dialog. Then, see if you can write the missing question. The response is given.

1. _____ ? Io ho dieci anni.

2. _____ ? Io sono dello stato del Colorado.

3. _____ ? Il mio nome è Sofia.

4. _____ ? Il mio nome è Enrica.

A.   The easiest way to ask a question in Italian is to simply raise your voice at the end of a sentence.

Sei italiana?   E tu?

B.   Another way is to invert the subject and the verb. (Put the pronoun after the verb.)

Come stai (tu)?

Quanti anni hai (tu)?

Qual è il tuo nome?

Now practice asking questions. Write a question using the method indicated (A or B), putting the words in the correct order.

Ex: English/speak/you   (A) Do you speak English?

1. are/you/American   (B) _____ ?

2. hungry/you/are   (A) _____ ? (familiar you)

3. are/hungry/you   (A) _____ ?

4. come/from where/ do/you   (B) _____ ?

5. you/do/eat/ breakfast   (B) _____ ?

6. you/what age/are   (A) _____ ?

ENTRARE
to enter

io entro	(ee-oh ehntroh)	I enter
tu entri	(too ehntree)	you enter
lui/lei/Lei entra	(loo-ee/leh-ee ehntrah)	he enters
noi entriamo	(noh-ee ehntreeahmoh)	we enter
voi entrate	(voh-ee ehntrahteh)	you (pl) enter
loro entrano	(lohroh ehntrahno)	they enter

Here are some other useful expressions with the verb *"enter"*:

Sofia entra nel cinema.	*Sofia enters the cinema.*
Loro entrano nel supermercato.	*They enter the supermarket.*
Noi entriamo nel caffè.	*We are entering the cafe.*

PARLARE
to speak

io parlo	*ee-oh pahrloh*	*I speak*
tu parli	*too pahrlee*	*you speak*
lui/lei/Lei parla	*loo-ee/leh-ee pahrlah*	*he,she,one (we speak)*
noi parliamo	*noh-ee pahrleeahmoh*	*we speak*
voi parlate	*voh-ee pahrlahteh*	*you speak*
loro parlano	*lohroh pahrlahnoh*	*they speak*

CHAPTER 4

(kooahntoh kohstah)
Quanto costa?
How much is it?

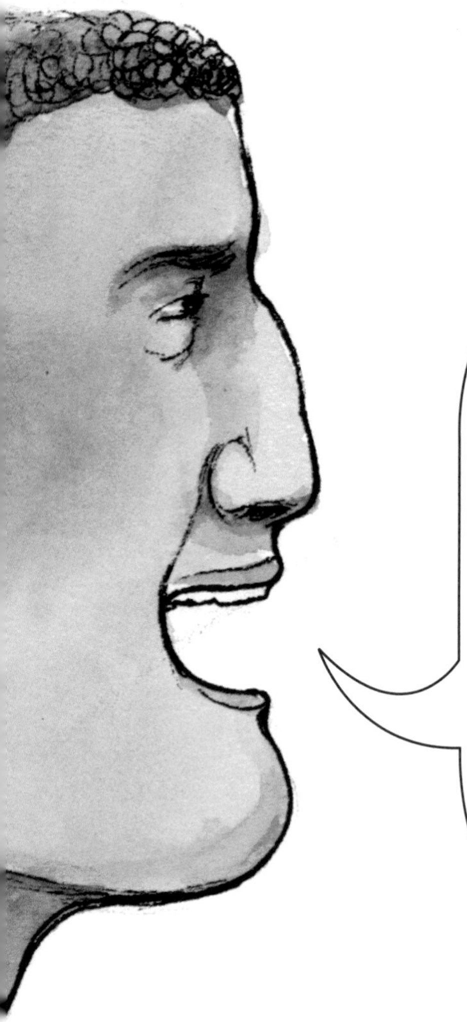

VOCABULARY

(keh kohzah)
che cosa
what

(mah)
ma
but

(lehntahmehnteh)
lentamente
slowly

(ehkkoh/prehgoh)
ecco/prego
There it is./You are welcome.

dahccohrdoh)
d'accordo!
OK!

(qooahntoh cohstah)
quanto costa?
How much is it?

VERBS

(cahpeereh)
capire
to understand

io capisco
tu capisci
lui/lei/Lei capisce
noi capiamo
voi capite
loro capiscono

(vohlehreh)
volere *(conditional)*
would like

io vorrei
tu vorresti
lui/lei/Lei vorrebbe
noi vorremmo
voi vorreste
loro vorrebbero

NEGATING YOUR ACTIONS

When negating Italian verbs, *"non"* comes before the verb conjugation:

Io non capsico *or* Non capisco
I don't understand

When using a verb negation with an object, Italians double negate:

Io non voglio niente *or* Non voglio niente
I don't want anything
(literally saying "I don't want nothing")

TITLES AND ADDRESS SYSTEMS

In Italy, people are very warm and friendly, yet one maintains a certain degree of formality when addressing those who are not intimates. Titles are frequently used:
Signore – Mr.   *Signor Rossi* (drop the ending "e" when attaching a name after)
Signora – Mrs.   *Signora Rossi* (keep the ending "a" when attaching a name after)
Signorina – Miss   *Signorina Rossi* (only used for young females. Be careful not to use this to address women with notable titles such as *"Dottoressa"*. *Signorina* is generally used to insinuate youth or being single)

In Italy, when one does not know someone, people use a formal case of "you".
For instance, in the grocery store or at work, *"Lei"* is used instead of *"tu"*. Note that *"Lei"* is always capitalized in order to distinguish between "she" – *"lei"*, and "you" – *"Lei"*.

Verb conjugations for "Lei" are third person, singular:
Lei vorrebbe qualcosa, signore? *Would you like something, Sir?*
Che cosa vorrebbe Lei, signora? *What would you like, Madam?*

BE POLITE!

Courtesy is important in the Italian culture.
It is good to remember to add courteous words especially to the beginning and ending of any request.

Noi vorremmo un'acqua minerale per favore.
We would like a mineral water, please.

Niente
nothing

Qualcosa
something

Io non vorrei niente.
I would not like anything.

Io vorrei qualcosa.
I would like something.

(pair fah vohreh)
per favore/prego.
Please/What would you like?

(see pehr fahvohreh)
sì, per favore
Yes, please.

(grahtsee-eh meeleh)
grazie mille.
Thank you very much.
Thanks a million.

(noh grahtsee-eh)
no grazie
No thank you.

(prehgoh)
prego.
You're welcome.

(ahrreevehdehrchee)
arrivederci!
Good bye!

STORY

It is 10:00 in the morning.

Isabella e Gianni are in Firenze.

Isabella is italiana. Gianni is americano

but lui parla un po' d'italiano.
he speaks a little

They are in una pasticceria.
pastry shop

Venditrice: Buon giorno signori.

Isabella: Buon giorno signora.

Gianni: Buon giorno signora.

Venditrice: Prego?

Isabella: Io vorrei del pane per favore.

Venditrice: E Lei, signore? Che cosa vuole?

Gianni: Io non capisco. Parli lentamente per favore.

Venditrice: Prego signori.
Here you are

Isabella: Lei ha l'acqua minerale?
mineral water

Venditrice: Certamente, signorina. Prego.
Of course

Isabella: Grazie signora. Quanto costa?

Venditrice: Tre Euro, per favore.

Isabella: Ecco tre Euro.

Venditrice: D' accordo.E Lei, che cosa vuole?

Gianni: Io vorrei due paste per favore.

Venditrice: Grazie signorina.

Isabella: Grazie a Lei signora.

Gianni e Isabella: Arrivederci signora.

Venditrice: Arrivederci, signori.

DO YOU UNDERSTAND?

Read the previous dialog carefully and see if you can answer these questions.
Check your answers in the back of the book.

1. Who is italiana in this dialog? _____

2. Why doesn't Gianni understand? _____

3. What does Gianni want to buy? _____

4. Who asks for mineral water? _____

5. Where does this scene take place? _____

I NUMERI 11 - 22

When saying a number in Italian, the accent is emphasized on the syllable immediately preceeding the *"dici"* portion of the word:

undici   oon'dici

quattordici   kooahtohr'dici

Notice that when a *"tre"* is added to the end of a number such as *"ventitré"* or *"settantatré"*, the *"e"* of *"tre"* is accented. But when *"tre"* is by itself or at the beginning of the number (i.e. *"tredici"*), there is no accent.

11	12	13	14	15	16
(oondeechee)	*(dohdeechee)*	*(trehdeechee)*	*(kooahttohrdeechee)*	*(kooeendeechee)*	*(sehdeechee)*
undici	dodici	tredici	quattordici	quindici	sedici

17	18	19	20	21	22
(deechahsehtteh)	*(deechohttoh)*	*(deechahnnohveh)*	*(vehntee)*	*(vehntoono)*	*(vehnteedooeh)*
diaciasette	diciotto	diciannove	venti	ventuno	ventidue

PREGO?

What would you like? or How can I help you?

NOTE: "Io vorrei" is the polite-conditional form of the verb "to want" and is commonly used, but it's always good to say "please" – *"per favore"* at the beginning or end of the sentence too.

In the following exercise, write the numbers in words, just for practice. Review numbers 1–10 in Chapter 2 if you need to. Say the numbers out loud as you write them. Then, practice saying each sentence with *"per favore"* at the end.

For example: *Io vorrei due paste alla cioccolata per favore.*

(Eeoh vohrrehee)   *(cahrtohleeneh)*
1. Io vorrei _____ cartoline.
    I would like   *11*   *postcards*

(too vohrehstee)   *(frahncohbohllee)*
2. Tu vorresti _____ francobolli.
   You would like   *18*   *stamps*

(Looee vohrrehbbeh)   *(beelyehtee)*
3. Lui vorrebbe _____ biglietti.
   He would like   *15*   *tickets*

(lohroh vohrrehbbehroh)   *(kahffeh)*
4. Loro vorrebbero _____ caffè.
   They would like   *3*   *coffee*

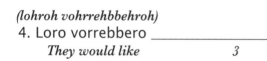

(Lehee vohrrehbbeh)   *(pehnneh)*
5. Lei vorrebbe _____ penne.
   She/You would like   *5*   *pens*

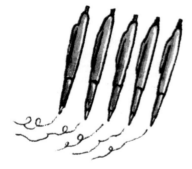

(vohee vohrrehsteh)   *(bohtteelyeh d'ahqooah meenehrahleh)*
6. Voi vorreste _____ bottiglie d'acqua minerale.
   You (pl) would like   *2*   *bottles of mineral water*

CHAPTER 5

(kooahleh johrnoh eh)
Quale giorno è?
What day is it?

(ahnnoheeahtoh/ah)
annoiato/a
bored

(eerahsheebeeleh)
irascibile
to be quick-tempered

VOCABULARY

(cohmeecoh/ah)
comico/a
funny/humorous

(lah dohnnah dahffahree)
la donna d'affari
businesswoman

(eel prohgrahmmahtohreh)
il programmatore
computer programmer

casa
house

(lah mahkkeenah)
la macchina
car

(lyee ohkee)
gli occhi
eyes

(Lah stehllah)
la stella
star

FOCUS : VERBS

NOTE: *piacere* is a special verb in Italian because it is a reciprocal construction, meaning it reflects back to the person. With *piacere*, this means one is literally saying: "it is pleasing to me:"

PIACERE
(peeahchehreh)
to like

mi piace/piacciono	*(mee peeahcheh/peeahchohnoh)*	*I like*
ti piace/piacciono	*(tee peeahcheh/peeahchohnoh)*	*you like*
gli/le/si piace piacciono	*(lyee/leh/see peeahcheh//peeahchohnoh)*	*he, she, one likes*
ci piace/piacciono	*(chee peeahcheh/peeahchohnoh)*	*we like*
vi piace/piacciono	*(vee peeahcheh/peeahchohnoh)*	*you like*
gli/a loro piace/piacciono	*(peeahcheh/peeahchohnoh)*	*they like*

An infinitive of a verb is the whole, original root, from which, in Italian three suffix endings are attached to differentiate if it is an *"are"*, *"ere"*, or *"ire"* ending verb.

Almost all infinitives stress the ending: *"ahbeeTAHreh"*. These are the simplest forms of Italian verbs.

ABITARE
(ahbeetahreh)
to live/reside

io abito	*(eeoh ahbeetoh)*	*I live*
tu abiti	*(too ahbeetee)*	*you live*
lui/lei/Lei abita	*(loo-ee/leh-ee ahbeetah)*	*he/she/you (fm) lives*
noi abitiamo	*(nohee ahbeeteeahmoh)*	*we live*
voi abitate	*(vohee ahbeetahteh)*	*you live*
loro abitano	*(lohroh ahbee'tahnoh)*	*they live*

STORY

Adamo e Maria abitano in una casa grande, blu e rosa.

Loro hanno un piccolo giardino con i fiori rossi e gialli.

Adamo è un programmatore di computer. Lui ha venticinque anni e ha gli occhi verdi.

In generale lui è molto simpatico, ma qualche volta lui è irascibile. Maria è una donna d'affari.

Lei ha venticinque anni e ha gli occhi castani. Lei è comica.

Per Adamo e Maria, èstato amore a
love at
prima vista.
first sight

Il lavoro di Maria è molto interessante.

A lei piace molto il suo lavoro.

Ad Adamo non piace il suo lavoro.
job
Lui è annoiato.

Adamo e Maria sono molto impegnati.

Ogni lunedì Maria va a Roma in treno.

Ogni mercoledì, Adamo va a Milano in macchina.

Ma ogni venerdì, Adamo e Maria mangiano insieme

in un ristorante chiamato "La Stella Rossa".

PRACTICE

Complete the following sentences. Use the vocabulary and the dialog to help you.

1. Adamo and Maria live in a big blue and pink _____ .

2. Adamo is 25 _____ .

3. In general Adamo is very _____ .

4. Adamo is _____ .

5. Adamo doesn't like his _____ .

6. Maria goes to Roma by _____ .

7. Adamo goes to Milano by _____ .

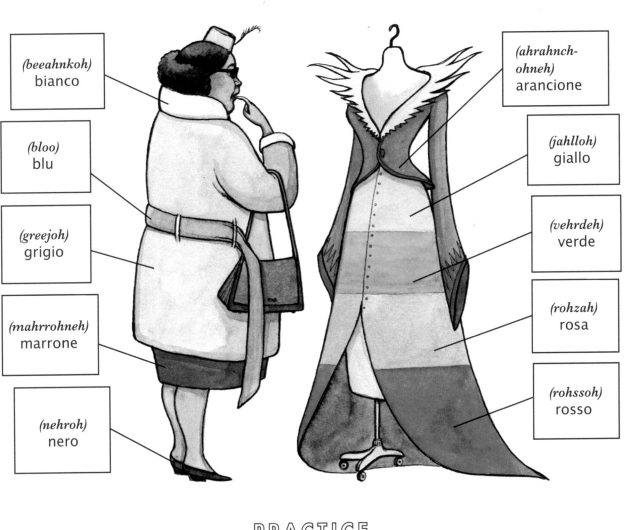

(beeahnkoh) bianco

(bloo) blu

(greejoh) grigio

(mahrrohneh) marrone

(nehroh) nero

(ahrahnch-ohneh) arancione

(jahlloh) giallo

(vehrdeh) verde

(rohzah) rosa

(rohssoh) rosso

PRACTICE

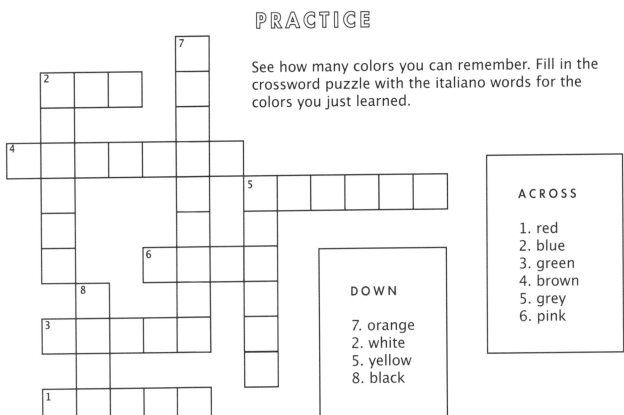

See how many colors you can remember. Fill in the crossword puzzle with the italiano words for the colors you just learned.

ACROSS

1. red
2. blue
3. green
4. brown
5. grey
6. pink

DOWN

7. orange
2. white
5. yellow
8. black

DAYS OF THE WEEK

(ee johrnee dehllah sehteemahnah)
I giorni della settimana

(loonehdeè)	*(mahrtehdeè)*	*(mehrcohlehdeè)*	*(johvehdeè)*	*(vehnehrdeè)*	*(sahbahtoh)*	*(dohmehneekah)*
lunedì	martedì	mercoledì	giovedì	venerdì	sabato	domenica
Monday	*Tuesday*	*Wednesday*	*Thursday*	*Friday*	*Saturday*	*Sunday*

Italians work five to six days per week, from Monday to either Friday or Saturday. It is not uncommon that an Italian works a six day week. Sundays, however, are sacred – so sacred in fact, that it is quite common to find many stores closed on Sundays. If you are planning to buy your groceries on the weekend or fill your car with gasoline, be sure to do these things Saturday!

Find *I giorni della settimana* hidden in the puzzle. Then circle them.

i'	d	r	e	n	e	v	s	g	l
d	o	m	e	n	i	c	a	i	u
e	e	r	c	r	z	e	b	o	n
t	d	n	u	l	m	p	a	v	e
r	n	r	c	z	g	p	t	e	d
m	c	s	c	m	q	u	o	d	i
m	e	r	c	o	l	e	d	i	m

PRACTICE

Put *I giorni della settimana* in their correct order by putting a number from 1 to 7 in front of each day.

_____ mercoledì   _____ domenica   _____ martedì   _____venerdì

_____ lunedì   _____ sabato   _____ giovedì

CHAPTER 6

Understanding directions in another language is particularly difficult, but not impossible!

Of course it helps to have **una mappa** so you can look at the names of the streets as
a map
the person you ask points to them. You don't have to understand every **parola**.
word

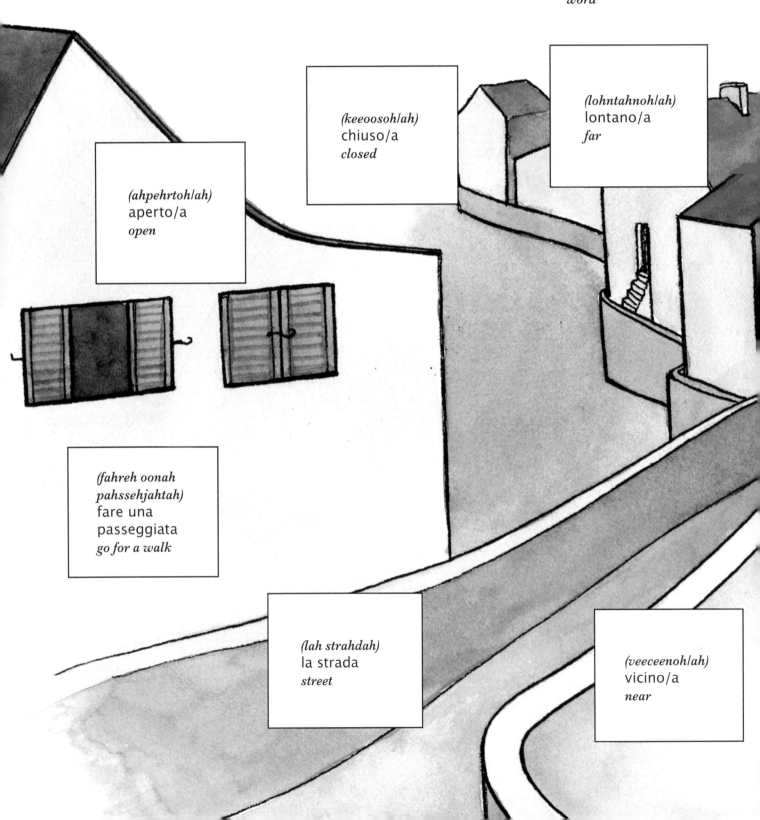

(ahpehrtoh/ah)
aperto/a
open

(keeoosoh/ah)
chiuso/a
closed

(lohntahnoh/ah)
lontano/a
far

(fahreh oonah pahssehjahtah)
fare una passeggiata
go for a walk

(lah strahdah)
la strada
street

(veeceenoh/ah)
vicino/a
near

LISTEN FOR THE VERB.
This will generally be the first word you hear because it will be in the command form: *diritto, camminare, prendere, andare, girare, andare diritto, attraversare.*

LISTEN FOR THE DIRECTION WORDS:
a sinistra, a destra, di fronte a

LISTEN FOR THE NAMES OF THE STREETS:
These will be the hardest to understand. (You can learn verbs and directions in advance, but names of people and places are more difficult because of the difference in pronunciation between English and Italian.)

(geerahreh)
girare
turn

vada diritto!
go up (a street)

(ahtrahvehrsahreh)
attraversare
cross

(eel pohnteh)
il ponte
bridge

When giving directions to someone, Italians use the verb as a command, or *un verbo imperativo*. The most common forms one uses in spoken Italian are *tu* – you, singular/informal, *lei* – you, singular/formal, and *voi* – you, plural/informal (now used often for the formal version as well). With this case, there is no need to use the subject pronoun beforehand (i.e. *tu, Lei,* and *voi*). Simply use the verb conjugation. Try the following commonly used verbs to give directions:

(dahlahltrah pahrteh dee)
dall'altra parte di
on the other side (of)

(veecheenoh ah)
vicino a
next to, beside

(dee frohnteh ah)
di fronte a
facing

(ah seeneestrah)
a sinistra
to the left

deereetoh)
diritto
straight ahead

(ah dehstrah)
a destra
to the right

(prehndehreh)
prendere
take
(tu) prendi!
(Lei) prenda!
(voi) prendete!

(ahndahreh deereetoh)
andare diritto
go up (a street)
(tu) và diritto!
(Lei) vada diritto!
(voi) andate diritto!

(ahndahreh)
andare
go
(tu) và!
(Lei) vada!
(voi) andate!

(cahmeenahreh)
camminare
walk
(tu) cammina!
(Lei) cammini!
(voi) camminate!

(ahndahreh deereetoh)
andare diritto
go down (a street)
(tu) và diritto!
(Lei) vada diritto!
(voi) andate diritto!

(geerahreh)
girare
turn
(tu) gira!
(Lei) giri!
(voi) girate!

ORDINAL NUMBERS

You will need to know ordinal numbers when someone gives you directions (telling you which *strada* to turn on). These numbers also come in handy when you need to tell which *piano* (floor) your room is on in your *albergo*.

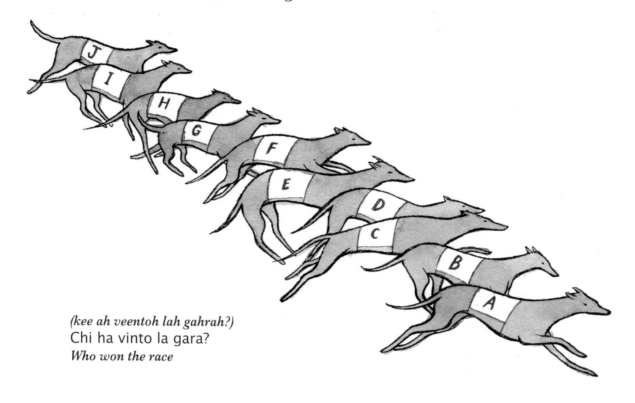

(kee ah veentoh lah gahrah?)
Chi ha vinto la gara?
Who won the race

Using the numbers on the right fill in the blanks to help the race announcer list the winner and the first nine runner-ups. Say each number as you write it.

A is _____	F is _____	*(nohnoh/ah)* nono/a	*(sehteemoh/ah)* settimo/a
B is _____	G is _____	*(qooahrtoh/ah)* quarto/a	*(ohttahvoh/ah)* ottavo/a
C is _____	H is _____	*(preemoh/ah)* primo/a	*(dehcheemoh/ah)* decimo/a
D is _____	I is _____	*(sehstoh/ah)* sesto/a	*(sehkoondoh/ah)* secondo/a
E is _____	J is _____	*(qooeentoh/ah)* quinto/a	*(tehrtsoh/ah)* terzo/a

DIALOG

Michele and Nicoletta are standing outside a hotel, talking. Draw the path that Nicoletta will take on the map below.

Michele: Dove vai oggi?

Nicoletta: Vado al cinema.

Michele: Ma oggi è lunedì. Il cinema è chiuso.

Nicoletta: Sì, hai ragione. Non importa! Dove vai tu?

Michele: Prima vado in banca. Dopo vado al parco, e poi vado a fare le spese al negozio.

                Vuoi venire con me?

Nicoletta: No grazie. Non voglio andare a fare le spese oggi. Vorrei andare al museo.

Michele: Puoi andare al museo Uffizi e Pitti oggi. Sono aperti il lunedì?

Nicoletta: Benissimo! Dov'è il museo Uffizi e Pitti? Sono lontani?

Michele: No. Non è molto lontano. Ci vogliono circa venti minuti a piedi.

Nicoletta: Caspita! È lontano... Va bene. È una bella giornata per fare una passeggiata.

Nicoletta: A sinistra in via Montagna, a destra in viale Cavour.

Michele: Prendi Cavour fino a quando arrivi al ponte.

                Attraversa il ponte e gira subito a sinistra.

Nicoletta: D'accordo. Giro a sinistra dopo il ponte.

Michele: Esatto. Vedrai il museo sulla tua destra.

Nicoletta: Grazie Michele. Ci vediamo dopo! Buona passeggiata!

Michele: Ci vediamo dopo! Buona passeggiata anche a te.

(cahpeeshee)
Capisci?
Do you understand?

Rispondi *"sì"* o *"no"*.

1. È chiuso il cinema il mercoledì? _____
2. Il Museo Uffizi e Pitti sono aperti il lunedì _____
3. Il museo degli Uffizi e il museo Pitti sono aperti il lunedì? _____
4. Vuole andare a fare le spese oggi Nicoletta? _____
5. È lontano il Museo? _____

CHAPTER 7

(kooahleh stahjohneh prehfehreeshee)
Quale stagione preferisci?
Which season do you prefer?

(eensohmmah)
insomma
in other words

(ahnkeeoh)
anch'io!
Me too!

(sehcohndoh meh)
secondo me
in my opinion

THE SEASONS OF THE YEAR

(leh stahjohnee dehllahnnoh)
Le stagioni dell'anno

Because Italy runs from North to South as a peninsula between the Meditteranean and Adriatic seas, the *stagioni dell'anno* bring weather of all types, depending upon the season. While in *l'inverno*, the Italian Alps up North are covered with *neve* (snow), the shores of Sicily are mild and moderately temperate. During *l'estate*, temperatures become intensely warm in the South all the way up to the *Dolomites* and the Alps in the North, where Italians take summer vacations in order to cool off in the mountain air. Italy enjoys four vivid and lovely *stagioni* throughout the year.

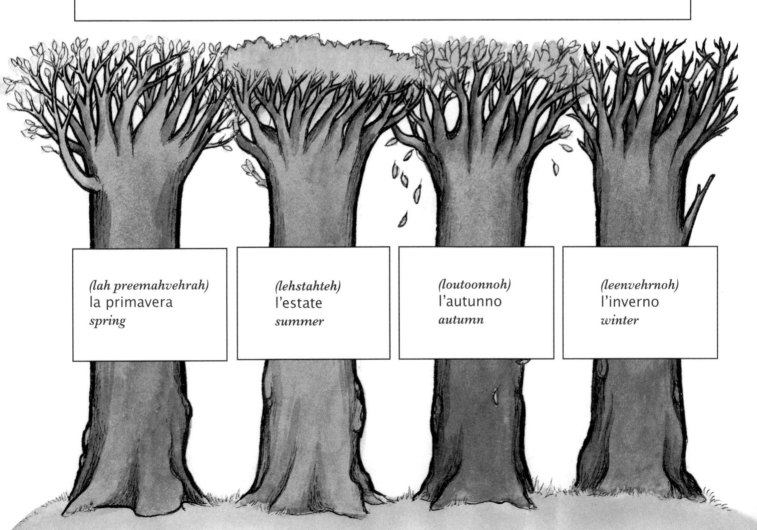

(lah preemahvehrah)
la primavera
spring

(lehstahteh)
l'estate
summer

(loutoonnoh)
l'autunno
autumn

(leenvehrnoh)
l'inverno
winter

THE MONTHS OF THE YEAR

(ee mehzee dehllahnnoh)
i mesi dell'anno

Months are not capitalized in Italian – except, of course, when writing them at the beginning of a sentence. Note that many of the months have double consonants ("*tt*", "*nn*"…so it is important to pronounce both letters by elongating your pronunciation of the letters:

settembre   *(seh̲t̲tehmbreh)*

Agosto is the favorite month of the year for most Italians because the holiday of *ferragosto* arrives. *Ferragosto* is when many Italians close up their homes for the month of *agosto* and go on holiday to relax and recuperate. What is your favorite month?

(jehnnaheeoh)
gennaio

(fehbbraheeoh)
febbraio

(mahrtsoh)
marzo

(ahpreeleh)
aprile

(mahjjoh)
maggio

(joonyoh)
giugno

(loolyo)
luglio

(ahgohstoh)
agosto

(sehttehmbreh)
settembre

(ohttohbreh)
ottobre

(nohvehmbreh)
novembre

(deechehmbreh)
dicembre

STORY

Look at the pictures and read the sentences under each one. See if you can figure out *il senso*. Write what you think the sentences mean in the blanks. Use the vocabulary and idioms on the previous pages to help you *capire* the story that follows the pictures.

(lah mahdreh)
La madre
mother

(eel pahdreh)
il padre
father

(lah sohrehllah)
la sorella
sister

(eel frahtehlloh)
il fratello
brother

(lah mahdreh een speeahjah doorahnteh lehstahteh)
La madre è in spiaggia durante l'estate.
during

_____

(Eel pahdreh een mohntahnyah doorahnteh leenvehrnoh)
Il padre è in montagna durante l'inverno.

_____

*(Eel frahtehlloh fah lahlpeeneesmoh
doorahnteh loutoonnoh)*
Il fratello fa l'alpinismo durante l'autunno.

_____

*(Leh sohrehlleh chehrcahnoh ee feeohree
doorahnteh lah preemahvehrah)*
Le sorelle cercano i fiori durante la primavera.

_____

(fahmilyah)

Il mio nome è Rosalba Simonetti. Io ho vent'anni. Ho una famiglia molto interessante.

(vahcahntsah)

Siamo tutti diversi. Quando andiamo in vacanza, mia madre vuole sempre andare in

(speeahjah) *(peeahcheh)(mohntanyah)*

spiaggia, ma a mio padre piace la montagna. Insomma, a mia madre

(spehcheeahlmehnteh)

piace andare in vacanza durante l'estate, specialmente in agosto. Mio padre preferisce

(peeahcheh)

l'inverno. A lui piace sciare in montagna a dicembre – dicembre o gennaio. A mio

(lahlpeeneesmoh)

fratello, Claudio, che ha diciassette anni, piace fare l'alpinismo. A lui piacciono

(kooeendee)

i colori dell'autunno (arancione, rosso, giallo, marrone). Quindi lui preferisce andare in
therefore

vacanza a settembre o ottobre. Alla mia sorellina, Genna, che ha quindici anni, piace la

primavera. Anche a me! Genna ed io amiamo tutti i bei fiori. Però, alla mia sorellina

non piace viaggiare. Secondo me, marzo, aprile, e maggio sono i più bei mesi per

viaggiare. Quando andiamo in vacanza? Tutto l'anno! Andiamo a fare l'alpinismo ogni

sabato a settembre. A volte andiamo a fare l'alpinismo durante l'inverno e la primavera.
at times

Certamente, andiamo a sciare per molti weekend a dicembre, gennaio e febbraio. A

giugno, luglio e agosto andiamo spesso in spiaggia. Stiamo anche a casa.

(ohnyoonoh)
Ognuno è contento.
everyone

PRACTICE

A. See if you can translate the following sentences into *inglese*.

   1. Mio padre preferisce l'inverno. _____

   2. A mio fratello Claudio, che ha diciassette anni, piace fare l'alpinismo.

      _____

   3. Quando andiamo in vacanza?

      _____

   4. A volte andiamo a fare l'alpinismo durante l'inverno e la primavera.

      _____

B. Now try to translate these sentences into italiano.

   1. I'm 20 years old. _____

   2. He likes the colors of autumn (orange, red, yellow, brown).

      _____

   3. Me too! Genna and I love the beautiful flowers.

      _____

   4. In June, July, and August we often go to the beach.

      _____

FOCUS

All Italian nouns are either masculine or feminine in gender. Sometimes it's easy to figure out which group a noun belongs to as in *un americano*, an American man, and *un' americana*, an American woman. Other times it just doesn't make any sense: *il programma (the program)* is masculine and *la Fiat (the Fiat)* is feminine.

Try to learn the noun markers *(la, le, il, i, l', lo, and gli)* together with the nouns: *la strada, il padre, la sorella, il fiore, le informazioni, gli uomini, una famiglia, un giorno.* This will help you a lot in remembering the gender.

When learning a noun, remember the singular and plural forms of the ending. Note that many regular nouns have rational ending changes: masculine nouns change from "o" to "i"; feminine nouns change from "a" to "e", and so on.

FEMININE
La stazione

MASCULINE
L'esame

There are 6 different ways of
saying "a" (the indefinite article):

una spiaggia
un'aquila *(an eagle)*
una strada *(feminine)*

un treno
un ospedale
uno zaino *(masculine)*

Choose the definite article that goes with these nouns.

1. _____ sorella

2. _____ spiaggia

3. _____ museo

4. _____ esame

5. _____ stazioni

6. _____ uomo

7. _____ fiori

8. _____ alberghi

9. _____ mele

10. _____ zio

Note: There are also masculine and feminine nouns that end with "e", which could take
either a masculine or feminine article. These must simply be memorized as having either
a masculine or feminine article:

L'esame (singular-masculine)   gli esami (plural-masculine)
La stazione (singular-feminine)   le stazioni (plural-feminine)

CHAPTER 8

(ehkkoh lah meeah fahmeelyah)
Ecco la mia famiglia.
Here is my family.

There is a good chance that if you make *un amico italiano* or *un'amica italiana*, you will be introduced to some of his or her family members at some point. Not only is it important to be able to understand these words that show family relationships, but it's also useful to be able to introduce and talk about the members of your *famiglia*.

(eel cahpehlloh)
il cappello
hat

(bahssoh/ah)
basso/a
short

(cohrtoh/ah)
corto/a
short

(eel mahreetoh)
il marito
husband

(lah molyeh)
la moglie
wife

(ahltoh/ah)
alto/a
tall

(ee kahpehllee)
i capelli
hair

(loongoh/ah)
lungo/a
long

FOCUS: FAMILY

MALE

Il padre	*(eel pahdreh)*	*father*
il nonno	*(eel nohnoh)*	*grandfather*
il suocero	*(eel soo-ohcheroh)*	*father-in-law*
il fratello	*(eel frahtehlloh)*	*brother*
il figlio	*(eel feelyoh)*	*son*
il nipote	*(eel neepohteh)*	*grandson*
lo zio	*(loh dzee-oh)*	*uncle*
il nipote	*(eel neepohteh)*	*nephew*
il marito	*(eel mahreetoh)*	*husband*
i genitori	*(ee gehneetohree)*	*parents*

FEMALE

la madre	*(lah mahdreh)*	*mother*
la nonna	*(lah nohnnah)*	*grandmother*
la suocera	*(lah soo-ohchehrah)*	*mother-in-law*
la sorella	*(lah sohrehllah)*	*sister*
la figlia	*(lah feelyah)*	*daughter*
la nipote	*(lah neepohteh)*	*grandaughter*
la zia	*(lah dzee-ah)*	*aunt*
la nipote	*(lah neepohteh)*	*niece*
la moglie	*(lah mohlyeh)*	*wife*
i parenti	*(ee pahrehntee)*	*relatives*

STORY

Pietro ha una piccola famiglia. Il nome di sua madre è Sofia. Lei ha i capelli corti e grigi,

(deenahmieekah)   *(mehttehrsee)*
e lei e' molto dinamica. Il nome di suo padre è Rinaldo. Lui è alto e a lui piace mettersi

i cappelli quando fa freddo. Pietro non ha sorelle, ma ha un fratello che ama

moltissimo. Si chiama Patrizio. Patrizio è molto comico ed e sposato con Luisa, la

(cohnyahtah)
cognata di Pietro. Lei ha i capelli lunghi e neri, ed è bellissima e simpatica. Loro non

hanno bambini. La moglie di Pietro si chiama Alessia. Lei è bassa, ha i capelli castani,

(soo-ohchehrah)
ed è molto intelligente. La suocera di Pietro è Elena e suo marito è Alberto, il suocero

di Pietro. Pietro e Alessia hanno una figlia unica. Lei si chiama Natalia. Lei ha undici

(spehcheeahlmehnteh)
anni e ama la sua famiglia, specialmente i suoi nonni. Natalia è molto energica. Infatti

(coh'rehreh) (johkahreh)
lei ha bisogno di correre o praticare uno sport al giorno. E Pietro? Lui è bello, ma non

molto intelligente.

48

PRACTICE

Fill in the blanks under each picture.
- a) Write the name of the person.
- b) Write what relationship that person is to Pietro. (Be sure to include the definite article.)

1. a _____
   b _____
2. a _____
   b _____

3. a _____
   b _____
4. a _____
   b _____

(Pietro)

5. a _____
   b _____

6. a _____
   b _____
7. a _____
   b _____

8. a _____
   b _____

FOCUS

See if you can answer these questions. Check your answers in the back of the book.

1. Chi e' molto intelligente? _____
   who
2. Chi ha i capelli corti e grigi? _____

3. Chi e' sposato con Luisa? _____

4. Chi ama i suoi nonni? _____

5. Chi e' bello? _____

POSSESSIVE ADJECTIVES

In general, in *italiano,* words that describe a noun – or adjectives – come immediately after the noun they are describing:

l'uomo alto   La donna bassa
The tall man   *The short woman*

It is important to remember if the noun it is modifying is singular, plural, masculine, or feminine, because the adjective ending will change according to the ending of the noun:

La figlia energica   Le figlie energiche

Certain adjectives come before the noun, including *piccolo* (small), and *brutto* (ugly):

i piccoli bambini   le brutte zie

There are also special adjectives which come before the noun and must be given additional attention, including *bello* (handsome) and *buono* (good). When *bello* and *buono* come before the noun, they must be conjugated according to the gender and number of the noun:

Bello…	Buono…
un bel treno – due bei treni	un buon piatto – due buoni piatti *(dishes)*
un bell'uomo – due begli uomini	un buon esame – due buoni esami
un bello zio – due begli zii	un buono stadio – due buoni stadi
una bella donna – due belle donne	una buona banana – due buone banane
una bell'arancia – due belle arance	una buon arancia – due buone arance
una bella zia – due belle zie	una buona zucca – due buone zucche

FEMININE		MASCULINE	
(meeah dzeeah)		*(mee-oh zee-oh)*	
mia zia	my aunt	mio zio	my uncle
(leh mee-eh dzee-eh)		*(ee mee-eh-ee zee-ee)*	
le mie zie	my aunts	i miei zii	my uncles
(too-ah dzee-ah)		*(too-oh dzee-oh)*	
tua zia	your aunt	tuo zio	your uncle
(leh too-eh dzee-eh)		*(ee too-oh-ee dzee-ee)*	
le tue zie	your aunts	i tuoi zii	your uncles
(soo-eh dzee-ah)		*(soo-oh dzee-oh)*	
Sua zia	your aunt	Suo zio	your uncle
(leh soo-eh dzee-eh)		*(ee soo-oh-ee dzee-ee)*	
le Sue zie	your aunts	i Suoi zii	your uncles
(soo-ah dzee-ah)		*(soo-oh dzee-oh)*	
sua zia	his/her aunt	suo zio	his/her uncle
(leh soo-eh dzee-eh)		*(ee soo-oh-ee dzee-ee)*	
le sue zie	his/her aunts	i suoi zii	his/her uncles
(nohstrah dzee-ah)		*(nohstroh dzee-oh)*	
nostra zia	our aunt	nostro zio	our uncle
(leh nohstreh dzee-eh)		*(ee nohstree dzee-ee)*	
le nostre zie	our aunts	i nostri zii	our uncles
(vohstrah dzee-ah)		*(vohstroh dzee-oh)*	
vostra zia	your (plural) aunt	vostro zio	your (plural) aunts
(leh vohstreh dzee-eh)		*(ee vohstree dzee-ee)*	
le vostre zie	your (plural) aunts	i vostri zii	your (plural) aunts
(lah lohroh dzee-ah)		*(eel lohroh dzee-oh)*	
la loro zia	their aunt	il loro zio	their aunt
(leh lohroh dzee-eh)		*(ee lohroh zee-ee)*	
le loro zie	their aunts	i loro zii	their aunts

Now see if you can put the appropriate possessive adjective in front of the following nouns:

1. _____ famiglia
   my

2. _____ casa
   his

3. _____ padre
   her

4. _____ sorella
   your (fam.)

5. _____ fratelli
   their

6. _____ cappello
   your (polite)

7. _____ amici (masc)
   my

8. _____ madre
   their

9. _____ moglie
   his

10. _____ genitori
    our

CHAPTER 9

(keh tehmpoh fah)
Che tempo fa?
What's the weather?

Being able to chat about *il tempo* (the weather) is a useful skill to have in another language. Whether you're at a bus stop, *nel ristorante,* or making small talk with a desk clerk at a hotel, *il tempo* is a safe, popular topic (and often necessary if you're planning outdoor activities).

Notice that the verb *"avere"* is used to express being cold: *"noi abbiamo freddo."*
The Italian language expresses people "having" a certain temperature instead of "being" a certain temperature, therefore *"avere"* (to have) is used as the verb instead of *"essere"* (to be), as it would be in English.

When referring to the weather, the verb *"fare"* is used: *"fa freddo"*. Literally translated this means "it makes cold." Of course, there are exceptions to this rule. Two exceptions are: *"è ventoso"* (it's windy) and *"è soleggiato"* (it's sunny). You will have to memorize the differences.

If you wish to say it is a little hot or warm, add a diminutive to the ending of the adjective: *"caldo"* will become *"caldino"*.

(fah cahldoh)
fa caldo.
It's hot.

(fah frehddoh)
fa freddo.
It is cold.

(eh vehnteelohzoh)
è ventoso.
It's windy.

(pee-ohveh)
piove.
It's raining.

(eh sohlehjjiahtoh)
è soleggiato.
It's sunny.

(fah behlloh)
fa bello.
It's beautiful.

(fah brootoh)
fa brutto.
It's horrible.

(nehveekah)
nevica.
It's snowing.

DIALOG

This is a telephone conversation between Elisa *e sua madre*. Elisa *ha ventidue anni* and is living in Alaska for 1 year doing research as part of her university graduate studies. *Sua madre* lives in Sicilia, where it is *soleggiato a volte e non nevica*.

Elisa: Buon giorno mamma.

Mamma: Ciao cara. Come stai?

(stoh ahbahstahntsah behneh, mah oh frehddoh)
Elisa: Sto abbastanza bene, ma ho freddo!

(pohvehrah feelyah. Cheh lah nehveh)
Mamma: Povera figlia. C'è la neve?

Elisa: Mamma, è inverno e sono in Alaska. Certo! C'è molta neve qui.

(cohmeh' eel tehmpoh een seecheelyah)
Com'è il tempo in Sicilia?

Mamma: Piove molto oggi, ma ieri è stato soleggiato. Infatti, faceva molto caldo ieri, ma oggi fa freddino. Domani ci sarà il sole di nuovo. Quando vieni a casa?

(sohnoh mohltoh eempehnyahtah cohn
Elisa: Non lo so. Sono molto impegnata con

lah mee-ah reechehrkah)
la mia ricerca. Lavoro ogni giorno anche la domenica.

53

(kahspeetah)
Mamma: Caspita! Dove lavori?

Elisa: Volo a Sitka ogni lunedì e sto due giorni.

Vado spesso anche a Fairbanks in macchina.
(koo-ee)
È lontano da qui! Preferisco lavorare qui ad

Anchorage. Devo andare di nuovo a

Fairbanks questo venerdì. Quando vieni a

(trohvahrmee)
trovarmi?

(ahdehssoh)
Mamma: Caspita, non adesso! Non durante l'inverno! Lo sai che non mi piace la neve.

(kahldeenoh)
Voglio venire in Alaska durante l'estate quando fa caldino.

Elisa: Va bene. Sì, fa troppo freddo qui d'inverno.

Forse vado in aereo a casa per le vacanze.

Mamma: Che bell'idea! Vieni a casa, cara.

Come lo sai, c'e' il sole qui a volte e non c'e' la neve!

Elisa: Va bene, Mamma. Ci vediamo presto.

(kahrah)
Mamma: Ciao cara. Stai su di morale!

PRACTICE

See if you can answer the following questions based on the dialog.

1. Chi ha freddo? _____

2. Dov'è Elisa? _____

3. Dove piove? _____

4. Quando lavora Elisa? _____

5. Quando vuole visitare l'Alaska, la madre di Elisa? _____

   _____

See if you can match the numbers of each statement on the right to the appropriate picture of the person to make each statement true.

1. Lei dice che piove.

2. Lei ha freddo.

3. Lei lavora da lunedì a sabato.

4. Lei dice che non le piace la neve.

5. Lei va al lavoro in aereo e in macchina.

6. Lei vuole visitare l'Alaska d'estate.

7. Lei vola a casa a dicembre.

8. A lei piace lavorare ad Anchorage

PRACTICE

Che tempo fa?
What's the weather?

1. D'estate _____ .
   it is hot

2. Ad aprile _____ .
   it rains a lot

3. A novembre _____ .
   it's bad weather

4. A gennaio _____ .
   it snows

5. Di primavera _____ .
   it is windy

6. A luglio _____ .
   it's humid

7. Oggi _____ .
   it's beautiful

EXPRESSIONS FOR TIME

You may recall the words *"ieri"* (yesterday) and *"oggi"* (today) from Chapter 6 when you learned about giving directions. Now let's add *"domani"* (tomorrow) to your vocabulary. (Remember how *"Mamma"* described *il tempo* in Sicilia?

(ee-eh-ree)
ieri

(ohgee)
oggi

(dohmahnee)
domani

Here are some useful time expressions:

(lah sehteemahnah skohrsah)
la settimana scorsa
last week

(lahltroh ee-eh-ree)
l'altro ieri
the day before yesterday

(lah prohseemah sehteemahnah)
la prossima settimana
next week

(dohpoh dohmahnee)
dopo domani
the day after tomorrow

See if you can figure out which word doesn't belong in each of the series of words below. Write the words in the blanks.

1. caldo, estate, sole, neve _____

2. ieri, freddo, domani, oggi _____

3. molto, quando, dove, chi _____

4. lavora, visita, qui, va _____

5. giorno, settimana, anno, primavera _____

VENIRE
(vehneereh)
to come

io vengo	*(eeoh vehngoh)*	*I come*
tu vieni	*(too vee-ehnee)*	*you come*
lui/lei/Lei viene	*(looee/leh-ee vee-ehneh)*	*he/she/you(fm) comes*
noi veniamo	*(nohee vehneeahmoh)*	*we come*
voi venite	*(vohee vehneeteh)*	*you (pl) come*
loro vengono	*(lohroh vehngohnoh)*	*they come*

FARE
(fahreh)
to make/do

io faccio	*(eeoh fahchoh)*	*I make/do*
tu fai	*(too fah-ee)*	*you make/do*
lui/lei/Lei/ fa	*(looee/lehee fah)*	*he/she/you(fm) make*
noi facciamo	*(nohee facheeahmoh)*	*we make/do*
voi fate	*(vohee fahteh)*	*you (pl) make/do*
loro fanno	*(lohroh fahnnoh)*	*they make/do*

CHAPTER 10

(keh ohreh sohnoh pair fahvohreh)
Che ore sono per favore?
Do you have the time, please?

(ehssehreh di boo-ohnoomohreh)
essere di buon umore
to be in a good mood

(ehssehreh dee cahtteevoh oomohreh)
essere di cattivo umore
to be in a bad mood

(ehssehreheen ahnteecheepoh)
essere in anticipo
to be early

(ehssehreh een reetahrdoh)
essere in ritardo
to be late

(lah stahtsee-ohneh trehnee)
la stazione treni
railroad station

(beelyehttoh/ee)
biglietto/biglietti
ticket/tickets

(eel beenahree-oh)
il binario (platform)
track

(ahndahtah eh reetohrnoh)
andata e ritorno
round-trip

(eel meenootoh/ee)
il minuto/i minuti
minute/minutes

(ahcheedehntee)
accidenti!
Darn!

DIALOG

Antonio e Carola arrivano alla stazione.
Viaggiano in treno da Roma a Milano per visitare gli amici.

(pehr cohrtehzee-ah, mee pohtrehbbeh deereh koo-ahndoh pahrteh eel prohsseemoh trehnoh...)
Antonio: Per cortesia, mi potrebbe dire quando parte il prossimo treno per Milano?

(pahreteh ahlleh dee-ehchee eh deecheeannohveh)
Agente di viaggio: Parte alle dieci e diciannove.

(ah keh ohreh)
Antonio: Scusi? A che ora?

Agente di viaggio: Alle dieci e diciannove, signore.

Antonio: Che ore sono adesso per favore?

Agente di viaggio: Sono le dieci e sedici. Lei ha tre minuti.

Antonio dice a Carola: Ci sarà un treno tra tre minuti! Siamo in ritardo.

Antonio: È sempre la stessa storia. Siamo sempre in ritardo.

Carola: Sei di cattivo umore stamattina, vero?

Antonio: Basta!

Carola *(all' Agente di viaggio)* : A che ore parte il prossimo treno per Milano? Non possiamo prendere questo treno purtroppo.

Agente di viaggio: Vediamo…il prossimo treno per Milano parte alle tredici.

(forte)
Antonio: Forte.

Carola *(all' Agente di viaggio)* : Va bene. Due biglietti per favore.

Carola guarda Antonio.

Agente di viaggio: Andata o andata e ritorno?

Carola: Andata e ritorno per favore. Classe seconda.

Agente di viaggio: Sono trenta Euro. Ecco i vostri biglietti.

Carola: Grazie. Quale binario?

Agente di viaggio: Binario otto.

Carola: Con piacere! È straordinario. Tu sei di buon umore adesso!

Antonio: Certo. Perchè non siamo in ritardo adesso. Siamo in anticipo! Andiamo!

DO YOU UNDERSTAND?

Answer "True" or "False" to the following statements based on the dialog.

1. Antonio e Carola viaggiano in aereo. _____
   plane

2. Antonio chiede che ore sono. _____
   asks

3. Antonio pensa che Carola è di buon umore. _____
   thinks

4. Carola chiede tre biglietti. _____

5. Loro viaggiano andata e ritorno. _____

WHAT TIME IS IT?

(keh ohreh sohnoh)
Che ore sono?

Expressing time in *italiano* is easy.

In *italiano*, it's important to say "in the morning," "in the evening", etc. when using the 12-hour clock, unless it's clear from the context that it's a.m. or p.m.

Sono le sette di mattina.   È mezzanotte.   Sono le quindici di pomeriggio.   Sono le venti di sera

(dee mahtteenah)
di mattina
in the morning

(mehdzohjohrnoh)
mezzogiorno
noon

(dee pohmehreejoh)
di pomeriggio
in the afternoon

(dee sehrah)
di sera
in the evening

To add the minutes, just add the number:

 Sono le undici e quaranta di mattina

 Sono le sette e venti di mattina

 Sono le quattordici e cinquanta di pomeriggio

 Sono le nove e mezzo di mattina

In Italia, the 24-hour system of telling time ("military" time as we call it in the U.S.) is usually used on TV and radio, with travel schedules, appointments, theater and concert times in order to avoid ambiguity. Just subtract 12 to figure out the time you are familiar with in the U.S. (16 hours is 16–12= 4 PM). In colloquial Italian, many people use standard numbers instead of military numbers, but this is when we use *"di mattina"* or other specifications to be sure that there is no confusion with the time of day being discussed. Therefore, one can say *"Sono le sedici"* or *"Sono le quattro di pomeriggio"* and both will mean the same time: It is four o'clock PM.

When saying the time in Italian, *"le ore"* (the hours) are said with the plural verb of essere: *"sono."* So when we ask *"Che ore sono?"* (what time is it?), the response is also plural: *"Sono le tredici."* (It is one o'clock). There are, of course, a few exceptions. When saying *"mezzogiorno, mezzanotte, or l'una,* the singular verb of "e" is used: *"È mezzanotte... È l'una di pomeriggio."* (It is midnight... It is one o'clock in the afternoon.)

PRACTICE

a. Sono le dieci e un quarto.
c. Sono le undici e trentacinque.
e. Sono le ventuno e quarantasette.

b. Sono le sedici e quarantotto.
d. Sono le diciassette e trenta.

1. _____ 2. _____ 3. _____ 4. _____ 5. _____

You'll need to know higher *numeri* if you want *capire i munuti* when someone tells you the time (...not to mention how important these numbers are for shopping or even revealing your age if the situation presents itself). Read the pronunciation carefully and say each number out loud.

Certain numbers, when combined with other numbers, are given different emphasis:

"tre":   *(vehntee)* venti 20   *(treh)* tre 3   *(vehnteetreh')* ventitrè 23

When *tre* is at the end of a number, it is given an accent at the end. If at the beginning of the number, then *tre* remains the same: *tredici*

Though an accent is not present, the emphasis is still on the first syllable.

"l'una": When speaking of "one" in expressing time, *"l'una"* is constant.
One would not say *"l'uno."*

23	ventitrè	*(vehnteetreh')*	40	quaranta	*(kooahrahntah)*
24	ventiquattro	*(vehnteekooahtroh)*	50	cinquanta	*(cheenkooahtah)*
25	venticinque	*(vehnteecheenkoo-eh)*	60	sessanta	*(sehssahntah)*
26	ventisei	*(vehnteeseh-ee)*	70	settanta	*(sehttahntah)*
27	ventisette	*(vehnteesehtteh)*	71	settantuno	*(sehttahntoonoh)*
28	ventotto	*(vehntohttoh)*	72	settantadue	*(sehttahntahdoo-eh)*
29	ventinove	*(vehnteenohveh)*	80	ottanta	*(ohttahntah)*
30	trenta	*(trehntah)*	90	novanta	*(nohvahntah)*
31	trentuno	*(trehntoonoh)*	95	novantacinque	*(nohvahntahcheenkoo-eh)*
32	trentadue	*(trehntahdoo-eh)*	100	cento	*(chehntoh)*

CHAPTER 11

(keh kohsah fahee doorahnteh eel too-oh tehmpoh leebehroh)
Che cosa fai durante il tuo tempo libero?
What do you do in your free time?

(ehssehreh mahneeahkoh dehllah prehcheezeeohneh)
Essere maniaco della precisione...
neat as a pin

(ahllahlbah)
all'alba
crack of dawn

(oonoh shehf dee ahltah koocheenah)
uno chef di alta cucina
a real gourmet cook

FOCUS: PREPOSITIONS

(een)
in
in

(davahntee ah)
d'avanti a
in front of

(sohttoh)
sotto
under

(dehntroh)
dentro
inside

(soo)
su
on

(dee-ehtroh)
dietro
behind

(foo-ohree)
fuori
outside

(veecheenoh ah)
vicino a
next to

USEFUL EXPRESSIONS

(nahveegahreh leentehrneht)
navigare in Internet
surf the Web

(mahndahreh oon email)
mandare un email
send email

(chee eh/cheh/chee sohnoh)
Ci e' (c'e')/ci sono
there is/there are

VOCABULARY

(ahl peeahnoh dee sohttoh)
al piano di sotto
downstairs

(ahl pee-ahnoh dee sohprah)
al piano di sopra
upstairs

(eel cahneh)
il cane
dog

(lah pehrsohnah)
la persona
person

(johvahneh)
giovane
young

(eel kohmpeeootehr)
il computer
computer

(eel gahttoh)
il gatto
cat

(vehkkee-oh/ah)
vecchio/a
old

STORY

Rocco è un piccolo cane marrone. Lui abita in una casa con un gatto nero chiamato Male.

Ci sono anche tre persone che abitano nella casa: una donna, un uomo vecchio, e un

giovane ragazzo.

La loro casa è bellissima e in ordine.

Rocco visita spesso Luca, un ragazzo di sette anni,

nella sua camera da letto al piano di sopra.

A Rocco piace sedere sul letto mentre Luca gioca

(johkahttohlee)
con i suoi giocattoli. Male, il gatto, dorme sotto
           toys

il letto.

Al nonno di Luca, Tommaso, piace passare il tempo

in cucina. Ama cucinare. Infatti, lui è uno chef di alta

       (fohrnoh)
cucina. A Rocco piace sedere vicino al forno e sentire

  (dehleetseeohzzoh)   *(tahppehtoh)*
l'odore del cibo delizioso. Male dorme sul tappeto avanti alla finestra.
                  rug

A Rocco piace dormire tutta la mattina ma la mamma di Luca, Caterina

si sveglia all'alba, va al piano di sotto all'ufficio e accende il computer.

Lei legge le sue email e naviga sull'Internet.

(lahvahndehreeah)
Male dorme nella lavanderia.
laundry room

A Caterina piace anche leggere le novelle e fare

(jahrdeenahjjoh)
giardinaggio durante il suo tempo libero.
gardening

A Luca piace suonare il pianoforte. Rocco si nasconde dietro il divano nel salotto

(roomohree)
quando Luca suona il pianoforte. A Male non piacciono i rumori. Quindi lui va fuori
noises

E dorme nel giardino.

Quasi ogni venerdì sera, Tommaso,

Caterina e Luca vanno al piano di sopra a

guardare la TV, leggere o giocare a carte

in salotto.

Male dorme nella poltrona e Rocco

(pahveemehntoh)
siede sul pavimento vicino alla sua famiglia.
floor

Rocco ha una vita abbastanza comoda.

DO YOU UNDERSTAND?

Che cosa gli piace fare? (What do they like to do?) Match the members of the family with the things they like to do. Write the letters in the blanks.

1. Rocco _____   A. suonare il pianoforte

2. Male _____   B. cucinare

3. Caterina _____   C. dormire

4. Tommaso _____   D. sedere sul letto

5. Luca _____   E. navigare in Internet

AMARE

to love

In Italian, the verb *"amare"* (to love) is a rather strong word. One uses *amare* when speaking of people they are romantically drawn to, or who are close family, or of food or objects they absolutely adore, whereas one uses the verb *"piacere"* (to like) when one is drawn to something or someone affectionately:

io amo	*(ee-oh ahmoh)*	*I love*
tu ami	*(too ahmee)*	*you love*
lui/lei/Lei ama	*(loo-ee, leh-ee amah)*	*he/she/you (fm) loves*
noi amiamo	*(noh-ee ahmee-ahmoh)*	*we love*
voi amate	*(voh-ee ahmahteh)*	*you (pl) love*
loro amano	*(lohroh ahmahnoh)*	*they love*

PRACTICE

Use the picture to help you fill in the blanks with *in, su, sotto, vicino a,* or *dietro.*

1.   Il ragazzo è _____letto.

2.   C'è un gatto _____letto.

3.   Il letto _____ tappeto.

4.   La finestra è _____letto.

5.   Ci sono dei giocattoli _____ letto.

Now write 2 sentences of your own describing the picture.

1.   _____.

2.   _____.

CHAPTER 12

(ahee pahssahtoh oon behl weekend?)
Hai passato un bel weekend?
Did you have a good weekend?

È lunedì mattina. Vincenzo e Monica lavorano per la stessa azienda.
(oofeechoh)
Vincenzo parla con Monica nel suo ufficio.

Vincenzo: Buon giorno, Monica. Hai passato un bel weekend?

Monica: Ciao, Vincenzo. Sì! Ho passato un bellissimo weekend.

(dahvehrro)
Vincenzo: Davvero? Che cosa hai fatto di bello?
oh yeah?

Monica: Ho giocato a tennis con la mia

sorellina sabato. Sabato sera sono andata a un
(fohrteeseemoh)
concerto – i Rolling Stones! Era fortissimo!

Vincenzo: Amo la loro musica. Sinceramente,

sono sorpreso che loro suonino.

Monica: Sì, loro sono vecchi, ma sono

(mehrahveelyohzee)
ancora meravigliosi.
marvelous

Che cosa hai fatto tu questo weekend?

(sehmpreh)
Hai giocato a calcio come sempre?
always/usual

Vincenzo: Ho giocato a calcio sabato e ieri

ho giocato un po' a pallacanestro. Ieri sera

ho guardato un film con mio nipote.

(veestoh)
Monica: Quale film avete visto?
saw

Vincenzo: Abbiamo visto il nuovo film di Harry Potter.

Monica: Sì? Era bello?

Vincenzo: Sì. Mio nipote, che ha otto anni, aveva un po' di paura, ma secondo me

(deevehrtehnteh)
era molto divertente.

(amusing)   *(rohmahnteechee)*
Monica: Mia figlia vuole vederlo, ma io preferisco i film romantici.

Vincenzo: Davvero? Anch'io.

(dah-ee)
Monica: Dai. Stai scherzando.

Vincenzo: No, davvero! Chiedi A Giulia. Lei sa che mi piacciono

i film romantici. Ciao! Vado.

Devo lavorare!

(ahspehttah)
Monica: Giulia? Aspetta! Dimmi di più di te e di questa Giulia!
wait
(sehgrehttee)
Basta con questi tuoi segreti!
secrets

(kohnvenyoh)
Vincenzo: Ci vediamo al convegno stamattina!
meeting

(greedahndoh)
Monica *(gridando)* **:** Accidenti! Quale convegno?
yelling   *darn!*

MATCHING

Match the questions and statements on the left with the appropriate responses on the right.

_____ 1. Era bello?

_____ 2. Ho visto un film ieri sera.

_____ 3. Stai scherzando.

_____ 4. Hai passato un bel weekend?

_____ 5. Come era il concerto?

_____ 6. Che cosa hai fatto questo weekend?

a) Sì, ho passato un bel fine settimana.

b) Ho giocato a calcio.

c) Era fantastico!

d) No, davvero.

e) Quale film avete visto?

f) Sì.

SIMPLE PAST TENSE VERBS

There are several past tenses in Italian, as there are in English. The *passato prossimo (pahsahtoh prohseemoh)* is commonly used as the past tense in Italian. It is a compound tense, which means it is made up of two parts: a helping verb *"avere"* (have) or *"essere"* (be) and a past participle *Sono andato*, (I went) *Ho pensato* (I thought), *Ho creduto* (I believed).

Most of the time in American English we don't use the helping verb. Instead of "I have eaten," we would say in English "I ate." The helping verb ("have"- ho- in this case) must be used in Italian: *Ho mangiato.* ("I ate.") The auxiliary/ helping verb changes according to the subject doing the action:

Avere verb: mangiare
io ho mangiato
tu hai mangiato
lui/lei/Lei ha mangiato
noi abbiamo mangiato
voi avete mangiate
loro hanno mangiato

Essere verb: andare
io sono andato/a
tu sei andato/a
lui/lei/Lei è andato/a
noi siamo andati/e
voi siete andati/e
loro sono andati/e

PENSARE
to think
Passato prossimo of pensare

io ho pensato	*ee-oh oh pehnsahtoh*	*I thought*
tu hai pensato	*too ah-ee pehnsahtoh*	*you thought*
lui/lei/Lei ha pensato	*loo-ee/leh-ee ah pehnsahtoh*	*he/she/you (fm) thought*
noi abbiamo pensato	*noh-ee ahbbeeahmoh pehnsahtoh*	*we thought*
voi avete pensato	*voh-ee ahvehteh pehnsahtoh*	*you thought*
loro hanno pensato	*lohroh ahnnoh pehnsahtoh*	*they thought*

With *essere* verbs only, notice that the past participle must agree with the subject. If the subject is feminine – like Monica – add an -a *("Io sono andata al mercato.")* ("I went." – That's Monica saying that.) If the subject is plural, add an -i (masculine or a combination of a male and female) *"Noi (Monica e Vincenzo) siamo andati al mercato."* ("We went.") If "we" refers to women and/or girls only, then it would be *"Noi siamo andate al mercato."* (with that extra "e".)

So, the past participles of *"essere"* act a little like adjectives since they agree in number and gender: For example: *lui è partito* (masculine singular for "he exited.")

To form the *passato prossimo* use the present tense of the helping verb plus a past participle. For verbs that end in -are in infinitive form (like *"andare"* -to go), just take off the -are from the verb *(andare)* and add -ato *(andato)* to form the past participle. For *ere* in infinitive form (like *"credere"* -to believe), just take off the -ere from the verb *(credere)* and add -uto *(creduto)* to form the past participle. For verbs that end in -ire in infinitive form (like *"pulire"* -to clean), just take off the -ire from the verb *(pulire)* and add -ito *(pulito)* to form the past participle.

FEMININE SINGULAR   lei è partita

MASCULINE PLURAL   loro sono partiti

FEMININE PLURAL   loro sono partite

ANDARE

Passato prossimo of andare (to go)

io sono andato/a	*(ee-oh sohnoh ahndahtoh/ah)*	*I went*
tu sei andato/a	*(too seh-ee ahndahtoh/ah)*	*You went*
lui/lei/Lei e' andato/a	*(loo-ee/leh-ee eh ahndahtoh/ah)*	*he/she/you (fm) went*
noi siamo andati/e	*(noh-ee see-ahmoh ahndahtee/eh)*	*We went*
voi siete andati/e	*(voh-ee see-ehteh ahndahtee/eh)*	*You went*
loro sono andati/e	*(lohroh sohnoh ahndahtee/eh)*	*They went*

PRACTICE

Choose one of these words to complete your *passato prossimo* verbs.

(noo-oh-tahtoh)
(avere) nuotato

(ahndahtoh)
(essere) andato/a/i/e

(mahnjahtoh)
(avere) mangiato

(cheeahmahtoh)
(avere) chiamato

(pehnsahtoh)
(avere) pensato

(pahrlahtoh)
(avere) parlato

(gooahrdahtoh)
(avere) guardato

(johkahtoh)
(avere) giocato

Ieri, io _____ alla mia amica.
1.

Noi _____ del weekend per molto tempo.
2.

Lei mi ha detto che lei era molto stanca sabato perchè

lei _____ a calcio tutta la mattina.
           3.

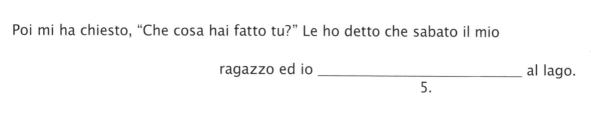

Quindi lei è stata a casa domenica e _____
                                              4.

la TV tutto il giorno.

Poi mi ha chiesto, "Che cosa hai fatto tu?" Le ho detto che sabato il mio

ragazzo ed io _____ al lago.
                        5.

Sabato sera noi _____ a una festa.
                          6.

CHAPTER 13

(keh kohsah voo-ohee mahnjahreh?)
Che cosa vuoi mangiare?
What do you want to eat?

(oh oonah fahmeh dah loopee)
ho una fame da lupi.
I could eat a horse.

(cheen cheen)
cin cin!
Cheers!

(boo-ohn ahppehteetoh)
buon appetito!
Have a good meal!

VOCABULARY

(oon teh')
un tè
a tea

(oonah beerah)
una birra
a beer

(oon cahffeh')
un caffè
a coffee

(eel veenoh)
il vino
wine

(eel lahtteh)
il latte
milk

(leh cheeleehjeh)
le ciliege
cherries

(lahnahnahs)
l'ananas
pineapple

(leh frahgohlleh)
le fragole
strawberries

(oon dohlcheh)
un dolce
dessert

(lah tohrtah)
la torta
cake

(leh mehleh)
le mele
apples

(leh bahnahneh)
le banane
bananas

(lah frootah)
la frutta
fruit

(eel gehlahtoh)
il gelato
ice cream

(lah crohstahtah)
la crostata
tart

(leh ahrahncheh)
le arance
oranges

(leh kahrahmehlleh)
le caramelle
candy

(leh pahtahteeneh freetteh)
le patatine fritte
French fries

(eel pahneh)
il pane
bread

(lah cahrneh)
la carne
meat

(eel pohlloh)
il pollo
chicken

*(eel mahntsoh)*il
il manzo
beef

(leh vehrdoorah)
le verdura
vegetables

(eel prohshootoh)
il prosciutto
ham

(ee peesehllee)
i piselli
peas

(eel pehsheh)
il pesce
fish

(leh cahrohteh)
le carote
carrots

(eel reezoh)
il riso
rice

(eel fohrmahjjoh)
il formaggio
cheese

(ee pohmohdohree)
i pomodori
tomatoes

(lah dzoopah)
la zuppa
soup

(leh oo-ohvah)
le uova
eggs

(leh cheepohlleh)
le cipolle
onions

(leensahlahtah)
l'insalata
salad

(ee foonghee)
i funghi
mushrooms

STORY

Tre amici sono al ristorante: Salvatore, Gregorio, e Enrico.

Salvatore: Che cosa volete mangiare?

Gregorio: Io non ho molta fame. Prendo della zuppa e dell'insalata.

Salvatore: E tu, Enrico?

Enrico: Io? Ho una fame da lupi! Non ho fatto colazione stamattina.

Salvatore: Davvero? Perchè no?

Enrico: *(zvehleeahtoh)* *(oh ahvootoh)*
Mi sono svegliato tardi. Quindi non ho avuto il tempo per mangiare.

Infatti ero in ritardo al lavoro.
woke

Gregorio: *(pehkkahtoh)*
Peccato!
too bad!

Cameriere: Prego signori?

to order
Gregorio: Che tipo di zuppa avete oggi?

Cameriere: Abbiamo minestrone.

Gregorio: Va bene. Buono. Vorrei della zuppa e un'insalata verde per favore.

(cohzee')
Cameriere: Basta così?

Gregorio: Sì.

Cameriere: E per Lei signore?

Salvatore: Prendo un panino e una caprese. *(cahprehzeh)*

Cameriere: Altro?

Salvatore: Sì, grazie. Per dolce vorrei della crostata per favore.

Cameriere: E per Lei signore?

Enrico: Allora, per antipasto *(ahnteepahstoh)* vorrei dei calamari fritti. Poi, per primo vorrei del

pollo *(pohlloh)* al marsala. Per dolce, *(appetizer)* vorrei del tiramisù.
chicken

Cameriere: Mi dispiace *(deespeeahcheh)* signore. Non abbiamo più il pollo. Abbiamo un piatto di
sorry

salmone al limone.

Enrico: Va bene. Prendo il salmone, grazie.

Cameriere: Vorrebbe un dolce?

Enrico: Sì, grazie. Vorrei del gelato alla vaniglia. *(vahneelyah)*
vanilla

Salvatore: Vorremmo anche una brocca di vino bianco della casa.

Cameriere: Benissimo.

Salvatore, Gregorio, e Enrico:

Cin cin!   Buon appetito!

PRACTICE

FOOD VOCABULARY

Use the clues in English to find the words in *italiano*.

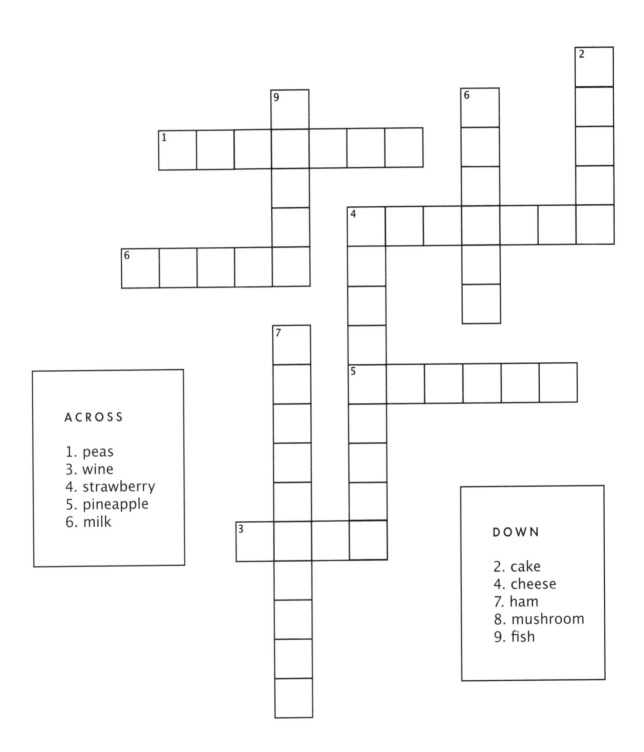

ACROSS

1. peas
3. wine
4. strawberry
5. pineapple
6. milk

DOWN

2. cake
4. cheese
7. ham
8. mushroom
9. fish

REVIEW

Vero o falso? *(true or false)*

1. Enrico ha molta fame. _____

2. La crostata di mele è un dolce. _____

3. Salvatore ha ordinato del vino rosso. _____

4. Enrico prende il pollo. _____

5. Enrico vuole del gelato alla cioccolata. _____

FOCUS:GRAMMAR

IL PARTITIVO - "SOME"

In *Italiano*, when saying "some" before an object, the preposition *"di"* is used, in addition to the correct conjugation of the according article:

Lei vorrebbe del pane.	*She would like some bread.*
Noi vorremmo della birra.	*We would like some beer.*
Vorreste delle arance?	*Would you (pl) like some oranges?*

di + il = del	del caffè	*some coffee*
di + l' = dell'	dell'olio	*some oil*
di + lo = dello	dello zucchero	*some sugar*
di + i = dei	dei funghi	*some mushrooms*
di + gli = degli	degli ananas	*some pineapples*
di + la = della	della cipolla	*some onion*
di + le = delle	delle fragole	*some strawberries*

CHAPTER 14

(kohsah cheh)
Cosa c'è?
What's the matter?

(sohno stahnkee - seemoh/ah)
sono stanchissimo/a.
I'm beat/I'm exhausted.

(boo-ohn cohmpleh-ahnnoh)
Buon compleanno!
Happy Birthday!

(kohsah cheh)
Cosa c'e'?
What's the matter?

(ahmahlahtoh/ah)
ammalato/a
sick

VOCABULARY

(chehlehbrahreh)
celebrare
celebrate

(oon rahffrehddohreh)
un raffreddore
a cold

(eel pehzoh)
il peso
weight

(lah sahlooteh)
la salute
health

DIALOG

Tre amiche si incontrano per pranzo a casa di Sara per celebrare il compleanno di Cristina.

Sara: Ciao Cristina. Buon compleanno!

Cristina: Ciao Sara. Grazie! Che bel giorno oggi. Ah! Mangiamo fuori?

Sara: Sì! Nel giardino.

Giulia: Ciao.

Sara: Giulia, cosa c'è?

Giulia: Non mi sento bene.

Sara: Peccato! Hai un raffreddore?

Giulia: Penso di sì. Ho mal di gola *(gohlah)* e sono
throat

stanchissima. Non mi sento di *(mee sehntoh)* lavorare.
feel

In fatti, non tornerò al lavoro questo pomeriggio.

Sara: Da quanto tempo sei ammalata?

Giulia: *How long (koo-ahzee)* Da due giorni quasi.
Since almost

Sara: Ma perchè sei venuta?
did come

Giulia: Perchè è il compleanno di Cristina!

Voglio aiutarla a festeggiare!

Cristina: Che simpatica Giulia. Grazie.

Giulia: Come stai Cristina? Tu sei stata molto ammalata lo scorso mese.

Cristina: Sto bene adesso. Guardatemi! Ho perso dei chili. Intoltre vado in bici
look at me!   *I lost*

ogni giorno al lavoro adesso.

Giulia: Fantastico! Guarda che bella che sei.

Come va il lavoro?

Cristina: Sono impegnatissima, ma è sempre molto interessante. Incontro

persone diverse ogni giorno.

Giulia: SPETTACOLOSO!

Sara: Venite a mangiare! Mangiamo l'insalata mista, l'ananas, il pane,

il formaggio, e la torta alla cioccolata per dolce.

Cominciamo con un bicchiere di spumante.

Giulia, Cristina, e Sara: Cin cin!

Giulia e Sara: Al quarantesimo compleanno di Cristina!

Cristina: E alla salute di Giulia!

(jah melyoh)
Giulia: Mi sento già meglio.
better already

SÌ O NO?

Read in *inglese*. Answer in *italiano*.

_____ 1. Does Giulia have a sore throat?

_____ 2. Does Cristina like her job?

_____ 3. Is the celebration at Giulia's house?

_____ 4. Is it Cristina's thirtieth birthday?

_____ 5. Was Cristina sick last month?

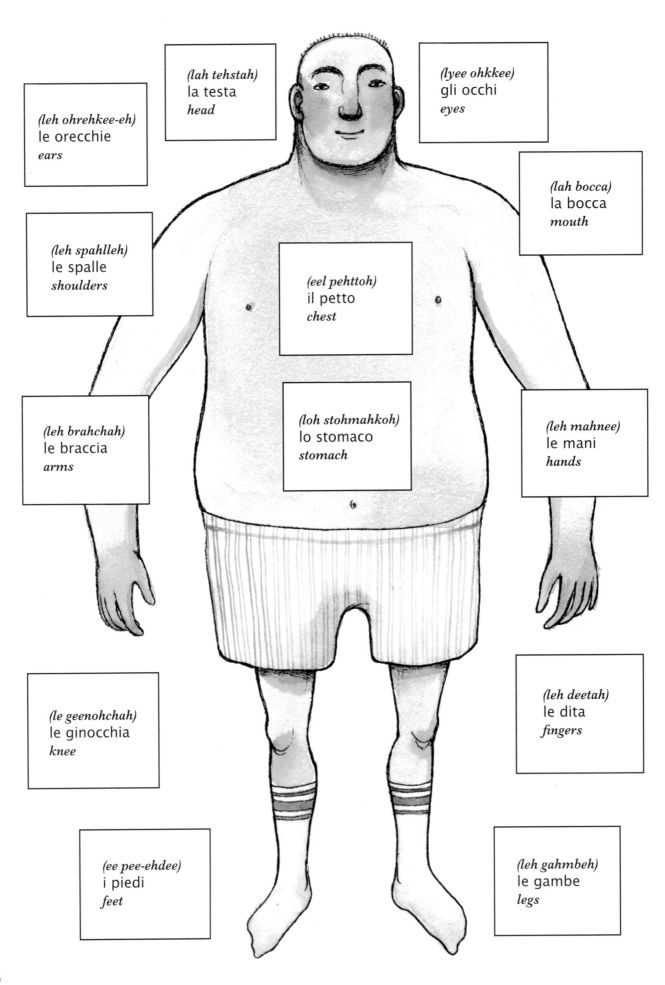

(leh ohrehkee-eh)
le orecchie
ears

(lah tehstah)
la testa
head

(lyee ohkkee)
gli occhi
eyes

(lah bocca)
la bocca
mouth

(leh spahlleh)
le spalle
shoulders

(eel pehttoh)
il petto
chest

(leh brahchah)
le braccia
arms

(loh stohmahkoh)
lo stomaco
stomach

(leh mahnee)
le mani
hands

(le geenohchah)
le ginocchia
knee

(leh deetah)
le dita
fingers

(ee pee-ehdee)
i piedi
feet

(leh gahmbeh)
le gambe
legs

86

PRACTICE

Avere mal di... to hurt

In *italiano*, when one says something hurts, the verb *"avere"* is used along with *"mal"* (abbreviated for male, or bad), the preposition *"di"* and the according body part:

Io ho mal di gola   *I have a sore throat.*
Lui ha mal di testa.   *He has a headache.*

"Avere" is also used to say that a body part hurts, so the verb *"sentirsi" (to feel)* is not used. Rather, *"avere"* is used. The idiomatic meaning of *"avere mal di..."* is *"to hurt."*

One can also use the verb *"fare"* to express pain, so long as the body part is the subject:

Le mie ginocchia / mi fanno male   *My knees hurt.*
La sua gamba / le fa male.   *Her leg hurts.*

Remember that Giulia said, *"Io ho mal di gola."* See if you can match *l'inglese* with *l'italiano* by looking at the diagram. Write the letters in the blanks.

1. Io ho mal di stomaco.	_____	a. My feet hurt.
2. le mie ginocchia mi fanno male.	_____	b. My eyes hurt.
3. Io ho mal di testa.	_____	c. I have a stomachache.
4. I miei piedi mi fanno male.	_____	d. My back hurts.
5. Io ho mal d'orecchie.	_____	e. My neck hurts.
6. I miei occhi mi fanno male.	_____	f. My knee hurts.
7. Il mio collo mi fa male.	_____	g. I have a headache.
8. La mia schiena mi fa male.	_____	h. I have an earache.

SENTIRSI
to feel

io mi sono sentito/a	*eeoh mee sohnoh sehnteetoh/ah*	*I felt*
Tu ti sei sentito/a	*too tee she-ee sehnteetoh /ah*	*you felt*
Lui/lei/Lei si è sentito/a	*looee.leh-ee see eh sehnteetoh /ah*	*he/she/you felt*
Noi ci siamo sentiti/e	*nohee chee seeahmoh sehnteeteee/eh*	*we felt*
Voi vi siete sentiti/e	*vohee vee see-ehteh sehnteetee /eh*	*you felt*
Loro si sono sentiti/e	*lohroh see sohnoh sehnteetee /eh*	*they felt*

CHAPTER 15

(tee vah behneh)
Ti va bene!
It fits you!

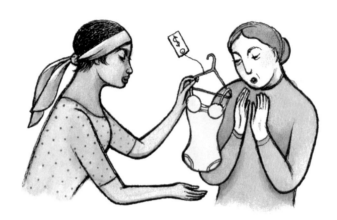

(dahee)
dai!
No way!

(nohn tee prehohkoopahreh)
Non ti preoccupare!
Don't worry!

(een zvehndeetah)
in svendita
On sale

VOCABULARY

(eel cohstoomeh)
il costume da bagno
swimsuit

(lahbeetoh)
l'abito
suit

(eel joobohttoh)
il giubbotto
coat

(ee pahntahlohncheenee)
i pantaloncini
shorts

(lah jahkkah)
la giacca
blazer

(lah fehlpah)
la felpa
sweatshirt

(lah bohrsah)
la borsa
purse

(leh kahltseh)
le calze
socks

(eel peejahmah)
il pigiama
pajamas

(eel vehsteetoh)
il vestito
dress

(ee kohlahnt)
i collant
pantyhose

(leh chabahtteh)
le ciabatte
slippers

(lah jahkkah)
la giacca
sports jacket

(lah sohttohvehsteh)
la sottoveste
slip

(eel rehjeesehnoh)
il reggiseno
bra

(ee jeens)
i jeans
jeans

(leh skahrpeh dah jeenahsteekah)
le scarpe da ginnastica
tennis shoes

(leh mootahndeh)
le mutande
underpants/undershorts

(dah dohnnah)
da donna
women's

(eel kahpehlloh)
il cappello
hat

(dah oo-ohmoh)
da uomo
men's

(lah sharpah)
la sciarpa
scarf

(lahbeetoh)
l'abito
suit

(leepehrmehahbeeleh)
l'impermeabile
raincoat

(lah jahkkah)
la giacca
blazer

(ee gooahntee)
i guanti
gloves

(la crahvahttah)
la cravatta
tie

*(lah gohnnah e
lah cahmeechah)*
la gonna e
la camicia
skirt and blouse

(l'ohmbrehlloh)
l'ombrello
umbrella

(lyee steevahlee)
gli stivali
boots

(leh skahrpeh)
le scarpe
shoes

89

DIALOG

(ahfahree)
Giorgio e Maria Carlino vanno alle Hawaii per affari e piacere. Vanno a fare
                                                        business   pleasure

(ahkweestee)(vehsteetee)   *(nehgohtseeoh)(ahbbeelyahmehntoh)*
acquisti di vestiti. Sono in un negozio di abbigliamento da uomo in questo momento.
shopping   clothes   store   clothing

Giorgio prova un abito grigio.
       is trying

                                   (pohrtoh)
Maria: L'abito ti va bene, ma io non porto abiti.
                                     bringing

Giorgio: Forse hai ragione. Questo è troppo formale per gli appuntamenti alle Hawaii.
             you're right

Maria: Mettiti questi pantaloni bianchi e questa camicia rosa.

Giorgio: Rosa? Dai! Dammi una camicia blu per favore.

(eel kohmmehssoh)
Il Commesso: Prego?
  salesman

Giorgio: Ha questa camicia in blu?

                   (meezoorah)
Il Commesso: La stessa misura?
                   size

Giorgio: Sì, grazie.

Il Commesso: Prego.

             (mehlyoh)
Giorgio: Molto meglio. Cerco anche una giacca sportiva.
             better

Il Commesso: Questa è in svendita.
on sale

Maria: Quella è alla moda. Guarda! Ti va benissimo quella, Caro!

Giorgio: Bene. Vorrei comprare i pantaloni, la camicia e la giacca.

(kahssah) (dee lah')

Il Commesso: Per cortesia, paghi alla cassa di là.
cash register over there

Adesso Giorgio e Maria sono al negozio di abbigliamento da donna.
women's clothing store
Maria prova un vestito giallo.

Giorgio: Quel vestito è bello ma è troppo lungo.

Maria: Forse sì... Signorina, Lei ha una taglia più piccola?

(Lah kohmehssah)
La Commessa: No, Signora, non abbiamo quella taglia.

Giorgio: Guarda questo vestito, Cara.

(ohrreebeeleh)   (mehttehr)
Maria: Quel vestito è orribile! Non posso metterlo.
horrible   wear

Giorgio: Non ti preoccupare. Non piace neanche a me!
I don't like it either

(loolteemah)
La Commessa: Le piace la gonna Signora? È l'ultima ed è nella sua misura.
last one

Maria: Mi piace molto quella gonna!

(mehtteetehlah)
Giorgio: Mettitela!
try it on

(sehtah)
La Commessa: Ecco una camicia gialla e una sciarpa di seta da mettere con la gonna.
silk

Maria: Va bene... Che cosa ne pensi?

Giorgio: Ti sta benissimmo!

(chehrkahreh)   *(sahrehmmoh prohntee)*
Maria: Benissimo! Andiamo a cercare i costumi. Poi saremo pronti per le Hawaii!
look for   *we will be ready*

   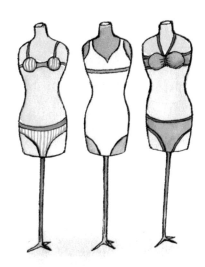

DO YOU UNDERSTAND?

Which of these statements describe the situations in the dialogs?
Put a check next to the sentences that are true.

1. _____ Giorgio compra una camicia rosa.

2. _____ A Maria piace la gonna.

3. _____ Giorgio si mette l'impermeabile.

4. _____ Giorgio e Maria vanno alle Hawaii.

5. _____ Giorgio dice che il vestito giallo è troppo piccolo.

DEMONSTRATIVE ADJECTIVES

Questo   questo/a *this*   questi/e *these*

questo cappello è rosso.	*This hat is red.*
questi cappelli sono rossi.	*These hats are red.*
questa gonna è grigia.	*This skirt is grey.*
queste gonne sono grige.	*These skirts are grey.*

When you are describing an object *(un cappello)* and you are demonstrating a particular object with *"questo / a / i / e"*, the demonstrative adjective must correlate with the object's number and gender:

"cappello" is masculine, singular, so it must take either *"questo."*
"cappelli" is masculine, plural, so it must take *"questi."*
"gonna" is feminine, singular, so it must take *"questa."*
"gonne" is feminine, plural, so it must take *"queste."*

When you are speaking with *"quello,"* and describing an object, quello is conjugated before the object with the according article:

quel giubbotto è bello.	*That coat is nice*
quell'accappatoio e' bello.	*That bathrobe is nice.*
quello stivale è bello.	*That boot is nice.*
quei giubbotti sono belli.	*Those coats are nice.*
quegli accappatoi sono belli.	*Those bathrobes are nice.*
quegli stivali sono belli.	*Those boots are nice.*

CHAPTER 16

(eh cozee lah veetah)
È così la vita!
That's life!

No matter how much *ti* prepare for *un viaggio* to a foreign country, there will often be some unexpected things that can happen. When some of these things are unfortunate or unpleasant, it helps to know some of *la lingua* in order to *capire* what people (like *dottori* or *polizia*) are asking. *Tu* might *anche* need *spiegare* what happened. A good attitude goes a long way in preparing *ti* to cope with unfortunate circumstances. Accepting an unforeseen event as part of *la tua esperienza* will help *ti* get through it. You will see in the story in this chapter how Robert, from New York, handles his *problemi* on a business trip to *Torino*.

(keh ohrreebeeleh)
che orribile!
What a terrible thing!

(mehlyoh) (keh mah-ee)
meglio tardi che mai!
Better late than never!

VOCABULARY

(eel kohmpeeoootehr)
il computer
computer

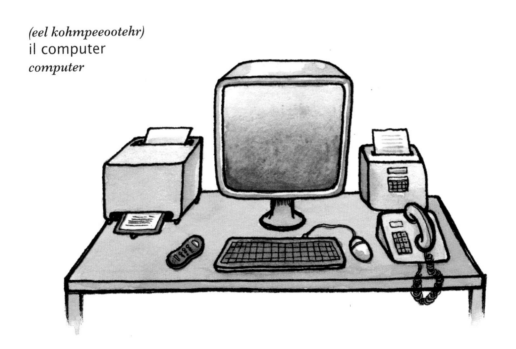

il telefonino
cell phone

la tastiera
keyboard

il mouse
mouse

(keh kohsah eh soochehssoh)   *(veeahjoh)*

Read *che cosa è successo* to Roberto on a *viaggio* to *Torino*.
what happened

(fohrtoonahtoh)   *(veeahjoh dahffahree)*

Mio fratello Roberto non è fortunato. Lui è andato in viaggio d'affari a Torino il
fortunate   *business trip*

mese scorso. Prima, il suo computer è stato rubato all'aeroporto. Che orribile!

(chehrkahtoh)   *(soopehreeohreh)*

Poi, lui ha cercato di mandare un fax al suo ufficio a New York, ma il suo superiore non
sought   *boss*

(lahshahreh)

l'ha ricevuto. Dopo, Roberto ha cercato di lasciare un messaggio
to leave

(sehcrehtahreeah)   *(foontseeohnahvah)*

sulla segreteria, al lavoro, ma non funzionava.
answering machine   *functioning*

(pehrsoh)

Il giorno dopo lui è arrivato a Torino; Roberto era molto arrabbiato perchè si è perso
                                             upset   *got lost*

ed era quaranta minuti in ritardo per il suo primo appuntamento. Quando qualcuno all'

appuntamento ha detto, "Meglio tardi che mai!" Roberto non ha capito che cosa

(vohlehvah)   *(ahl eeneezeeoh)*   *(see sehnteevah)*

voleva dire l'uomo all'inizio. Dopo che lui ha capito, si sentiva un po' meglio.
wanting   *at first*   *felt*

(ahlmehnoh)   *(kahpahcheh)*

Almeno Roberto era capace di mandare un email al suo superiore, alla sua famiglia (ed a

me), e agli amici. Lui ha trovato un caffè con l'Internet vicino al suo albergo, quindi ha

lavorato sui computer lì quasi ogni sera. Mio fratello ha detto che c'erano sempre molte

(stahvahnoh mahndahndoh)

persone al caffè con l'Internet che stavano mandando email, navigavano l'Internet e

were sending

usavano in generale i computer. Roberto non poteva scrivere a macchina

couldn't   type

(pehroh')   *(lah tahstee-ehrah)*

velocemente però, perchè la tastiera era diversa. Una sera, lui ha rovesciato il caffè sul

mouse e sulla tastiera e il proprietario non era molto felice. Che errore!

owner

Poi, sabato, una mattina soleggiata Roberto ha affittato una macchina e ha guidato verso la

(kahmpahnyah)   *(fee-oomeh)*

campagna per fare un picnic sul fiume.

countryside   *river*

(poortrohppoh)   *(sohrprehsah)*   *(rohttah)(soolowtohstrahdah)*
Purtroppo, ma senza sorpresa, la sua macchina si è rotta sull'autostrada.
                                        broke down on the highway

            (ahfeetahtoh)   *(pee-ohvehvah)*
Domenica, lui ha affittato una bici per andare al parco. Pioveva quasi tutto il tempo e
          rented   *rained*

          (gohmmah buhcahtah)   *(sfohrtoonahtoh)*
lui aveva una gomma bucata al ritorno. Povero Roberto! Però, anche se è sfortunato
       flat tire   *unlucky*

mio fratello dice sempre "È così la vita!"

DO YOU UNDERSTAND?

Match the phrases on the left with the words on the right.

1. "Meglio tardi che mai!" _____   a) sul mouse e sulla tastiera

2. il superiore non ha ricevuto _____   b) Dal caffè con l'Internet

3. si è rotta sull'autostrada _____   c) l'appuntamento

4. si è rovesciato il caffè _____   d) il computer

5. aveva una gomma bucata _____   e) la macchina

6. ha mandato gli email _____   f) la bici

7. era stato rubato _____   g) il fax

MATCHING

1. trovato _____   a) rented

2. affittato _____   b) stolen

3. perso _____   c) tried

4. capito _____   d) found

5. ricevuto _____   e) lost

6. arrivato _____   f) understood

7. rubato _____   g) arrived

8. rovesciato _____   h) received

9. provato _____   i) spilled

FOCUS

In Italy, if you have an emergency, there is information in the front pages of the telephone book. If you have a minor ailment and require a mild form of medicine, though in Italy, some over-the-counter drugs are only sold with a prescription, pharmacies are a good place to get help – even in an emergency. Be prepared to spend some time completing reports if you should be so *sfortunato* to have something stolen. Public Italian agencies are known for the paperwork and time involved in filing a report.

(lehmehrjehntseeah)
l'emergenza
emergency

(keh kohzah eh soochehssoh)
Che cosa è successo?
What happened?

(aheeoootoh)
aiuto!
Help!

(lohroh ahnnoh roobahtoh eel mee-oh)
Loro hanno rubato il mio…
They stole my…

(lahdroh)
ladro!
Thief!

(pohleetseeah)
polizia!
Police!

(ee-oh vohlyoh reepohrtahreh oon ahcheedehnteh)
Io voglio riportare un incidente…
I want to report an accident…

(foo-ohkoh)
fuoco!
Fire!

Find these 4 emergency words in the puzzle: *fuoco, polizia, aiuto, ladro*. Then circle them.

r	v	f	d	a	x	a	l	u	g
g	w	u	e	l	f	i	a	r	o
i	t	o	l	u	s	u	d	g	w
v	f	c	s	e	u	t	r	e	t
s	u	o	j	y	u	o	o	n	t
q	i	z	x	t	w	r	g	c	i
d	p	o	l	i	z	i	a	e	g

To build on the foundation this book provides, you should immerse yourself in Italian as much as you can. Listen to audiocassettes and CD's, interact with CD ROM products such as those from TOPICS Entertainment, which are good sources of authentic Italian speech. Italian radio and television programs may be available in your area. Italian films are another enjoyable way to hear the language. Read anything you can find in Italian, including children's books, easy novels, comics, magazines, newspapers, and even the labels on household products. Search the Internet for Italian websites that will give you countless opportunities to read and listen to Italian.

ANSWER KEY

CAPITOLO 1

Matching
1) A
2) F
3) C
4) B
5) E
6) D

CAPITOLO 2

Practice (numbers)
1) Tre più uno fa quattro
2) Sei più quattro fa dieci.
3) Due più tre fa cinque.
4) Otto meno cinque fa tre.
5) Nove meno otto fa uno.
6) Dieci meno tre fa sette.
7) Quattro per due fa otto.
8) Tre per tre fa nove.

Practice
1) Anna e la sua amica mangiano in un caffè.
2) Giulia ha due panini.
3) Giacomo entra nel ristorante.
4) Giacomo è felice.

CAPITOLO 3

Practice
1) Quanti anni hai?
2) Di dove sei?
3) Qual il tuo nome?
4) Qual è il tuo nome?

Practice
1) Sei americano/a (tu)?
2) Hai fame?
3) Hai fame (tu)?
4) Di dove sei (tu)?
5) Fai colazione (tu)?
6) Quanti anni hai?

CAPITOLO 4

Practice
1) La venditrice è italiana.
2) La venditrice usa il formale : Lei vuole sapere cosa vuole Gianni.
3) Gianni vuole comprare due paste.
4) Isabella chiede l'acqua minerale.
5) In una pasticceria.

Prego...
1) undici
2) diciotto
3) quindici
4) tre
5) cinque
6) due

CAPITOLO 5

Practice
1) casa
2) anni
3) simpatico
4) comica
5) lavoro
6) treno
7) macchina

Practice
1) lunedì
2) martedì
3) mercoledì
4) giovedì
5) venerdì
6) sabato
7) domenica

Puzzle

Down
7. arancione
2. bianco
5. giallo
8. nero

Across
1. rosso
2. blu
3. verde
4. marrone
5. grigio
6. rosa

CAPITOLO 6

Capisci?
1) no
2) sì
3) no
4) no
5) no

CAPITOLO 7

1) La mamma va in spiaggia durante l'estate.
2) Il padre va in montagna durante l'inverno.
3) Il fratello fa l'alpinismo durante l'autunno.
4) Le sorelle cercano i fiori durante la primavera.

1) My father prefers winter.
2) My brother Claudio, who is seventeen years old, likes to hike in the forest.
3) When are we going on vacation?
4) At times, we go hiking during the winter and summer.

1) la
2) la
3) il
4) l'
5) le
6) l'
7) i
8) gli
9) le
10) lo

CAPITOLO 8

Practice
1) Rinaldo è suo padre.
2) Sofia è sua madre.
3) Pietro è lui.
4) Alessia è sua moglie.
5) Natalia è sua figlia.
6) Alberto è suo suocero.
7) Elena è sua suocera.
8) Patrizio è suo fratello.
9) Luisa è sua cognata.

1) Alessia è molto intelligente.
2) Sofia ha i capelli corti e grigi.
3) Patrizio è sposato con Luisa.
4) Natalia ama i suoi nonni.
5) Pietro è bello.

1) La mia famiglia.
2) La sua casa.
3) Sua padre.
4) Tua sorella.
5) I loro fratelli.
6) Il Suo cappello.
7) I miei amici.
8) La loro madre.
9) Sua moglie.
10) I nostri genitori.

CAPITOLO 9

Practice
1) Elisa ha freddo.
2) Elisa è in Alaska.
3) Piove in Sicilia.
4) Elisa lavora ogni giorno anche la domenica.
5) La madre di Elisa vuole visitare l'Alaska durante l'estate.

Il tempo
1) D'estate fa caldo.
2) Ad aprile piove molto.
3) A novembre fa brutto il tempo.
4) A gennaio nevica.
5) Di primavera è ventoso.
6) A luglio è umido.
7) Oggi fa bello.

Practice and review
1) neve
2) freddo
3) molto
4) qui
5) primavera

CAPITOLO 10

Practice
1) falso
2) vero
3) falso
4) falso
5) vero

L'ora
1) Sono le diciasette e trenta.

2) Sono le ventuno e quarantasette.
3) Sono le dieci e un quarto.
4) Sono le undici e trentotto.
5) Sono le sedici e quarantacinque.

CAPITOLO 11

Practice
1) D – sedere sul letto.
2) C – dormire
3) E – navigare in Internet
4) B – cucinare
5) A – suonare il pianoforte

CAPITOLO 12

Matching
1) F
2) E
3) D
4) A
5) C
6) B

Practice
1) chiamato
2) abbiamo parlato
3) ha giocato
4) ha guardato
5) abbiamo nuotato
6) siamo andati

CAPITOLO 13

Puzzle
Across
1. piselli
3. vino
4. fragola
5. ananas
6. latte

Down
2. torta
4. formaggio
7. prosciutto
8. funghi
9. pesce

Practice
1) vero
2) vero
3) falso
4) falso
5) falso

CAPITOLO 14

Practice
1) Sì, Giulia ha mal di gola.
2) Sì, a Cristina piace il suo lavoro.
3) No, la festa è a casa di Sara.
4) No, è il quarantesimo compleanno di Cristina.
5) Sì, Cristina è stata ammalata il mese scorso.

Practice – Il corpo
1) C
2) F
3) G
4) A
5) H
6) B
7) B
8) D

CAPITOLO 15

Capisci?
1) falso
2) vero
3) falso
4) vero
5) falso

CAPITOLO 16

Capisci?
1) C
2) G
3) E
4) A
5) F
6) B
7) D

Matching
1) D
2) A
3) E
4) F
5) H
6) G
7) B
8) I
9) C

GLOSSARY

CAPITOLO 1

ENGLISH TO ITALIAN

a lot	–	molto
at	–	a
beach	–	la spiaggia
bed	–	il letto
breakfast	–	la colazione
brioche	–	la brioche
car	–	la macchina
dinner	–	la cena
(to) eat	–	mangiare
(to) have	–	avere
I	–	io
in	–	in
(a) little	–	un po'
lunch	–	il pranzo
man	–	l'uomo
me	–	mi/me
meat	–	la carne
morning	–	la mattina
on	–	su
pasta	–	la pasta
(to) say	–	dire
train	–	il treno
(to) want	–	volere
where	–	dove
woman	–	la donna
you (formal)	–	Lei
you (informal)	–	tu

ITALIAN TO ENGLISH

molto	–	a lot
a	–	at
la spiaggia	–	beach
il letto	–	bed
la colazione	–	breakfast
la brioche	–	brioche
la macchina	–	car
la cena	–	dinner
mangiare	–	(to) eat
avere	–	(to) have
io	–	I
in	–	in
un po'	–	(a) little
il pranzo	–	lunch
l'uomo	–	man
mi/me	–	me
la carne	–	meat
la mattina	–	morning
su	–	on
la pasta	–	pasta
dire	–	(to) say
il treno	–	train
volere	–	(to) want
dove	–	where
la donna	–	woman
Lei	–	you (informal)
tu	–	you (informal)

CAPITOLO 2

cheese	–	il formaggio
(to) enter	–	entrare
friend (fem)	–	l'amica
friend (masc)	–	l'amico
(to) give	–	dare
happy	–	felice
hungry	–	avere fame
(to) introduce	–	presentarsi
(to) leave	–	uscire/partire
(to) respond	–	rispondere
restaurant	–	il ristorante
sad	–	triste
sandwich	–	il panino

il formaggio	–	cheese
entrare	–	(to) enter
l'amica	–	friend (fem)
l'amico	–	friend (masc)
dare	–	(to) give
felice	–	happy
avere fame	–	hungry
presentarsi	–	(to) introduce
uscire/partire	–	(to) leave
rispondere	–	(to) respond
il ristorante	–	restaurant
triste	–	sad
il panino	–	sandwich

CAPITOLO 3

(to) be	–	essere
boy	–	il ragazzo
certainly	–	certamente
(to) come	–	venire
daughter	–	la figlia
girl	–	la ragazza
(to) have	–	avere
here is/are	–	ecco
no	–	no
of course not	–	certamente no
son	–	il figlio
(to) speak	–	parlare
thirsty	–	avere sete
tired	–	stanco
yes	–	sì

essere	–	(to) be
il ragazzo	–	boy
certamente	–	certainly
venire	–	(to) come
la figlia	–	daughter
la ragazza	–	girl
avere	–	(to) have
ecco	–	here is/are
no	–	no
certamente no	–	of course not
il figlio	–	son
parlare	–	(to) speak
avere sete	–	thirsty
stanco	–	tired
si'	–	yes

CAPITOLO 4

agreed	–	d'accordo
bottle	–	la bottiglia
but	–	ma

d'accordo	–	agreed
la bottiglia	–	bottle
ma	–	but

coffee	–	il caffè		il caffè	–	coffee
good bye	–	arrivederci		arrivederci	–	good bye
loaf of bread	–	il pane		il pane	–	loaf of bread
madam	–	la signora		la signora	–	madam
mineral water	–	l'acqua minerale		l'acqua minerale	–	mineral water
pastry shop	–	la pasticceria		la pasticceria	–	pastry shop
pen	–	la penna		la penna	–	pen
please	–	per favore		per favore	–	please
postcard	–	la cartolina		la cartolina	–	postcard
sir	–	il signore		il signore	–	sir
slowly	–	lentamente		lentamente	–	slowly
stamp	–	il francobollo		il francobollo	–	stamp
thank you	–	grazie		grazie	–	thank you
there you are	–	ecco		ecco	–	there you are
ticket	–	il biglietto		il biglietto	–	ticket
(to) understand	–	capire		capire	–	(to) understand
very much	–	molto		molto	–	very much
what	–	che cosa		che cosa	–	what
you're welcome	–	prego		prego	–	you're welcome

CAPITOLO 5

and	–	e		e	–	and
bored	–	annoiato		annoiato	–	bored
both	–	entrambe		entrambe	–	both
businesswoman	–	la commessa		la donna d'affari	–	business woman
busy	–	impegnato		impegnato	–	busy
by	–	vicino a		vicino a	–	by
Color	–	il colore		il colore	–	color
black	–	nero		nero	–	black
green	–	verde		verde	–	green
grey	–	grigio		grigio	–	grey
red	–	rosso		rosso	–	red
violet	–	violetto		violetto	–	violet
white	–	bianco		bianco	–	white
yellow	–	giallo		giallo	–	yellow
computer programmer	–	il programmatore		il programmatore	–	computer programmer
day	–	il giorno		il giorno	–	day
Monday	–	lunedì		lunedì	–	Monday
Tuesday	–	martedì		martedì	–	Tuesday
Wednesday	–	mercoledì		mercoledì	–	Wednesday
Thursday	–	giovedì		giovedì	–	Thursday
Friday	–	venerdì		venerdì	–	Friday
Saturday	–	sabato		sabato	–	Saturday
Sunday	–	domenica		domenica	–	Sunday
each	–	ogni		ogni	–	each
every	–	ogni		ogni	–	each
eyes	–	gli occhi		gli occhi	–	eyes
flower	–	il fiore		il fiore	–	flower
funny	–	comico		comico	–	funny
garden	–	il giardino		il giardino	–	garden
(to) go	–	andare		andare	–	(to) go
house	–	la casa		la casa	–	house
in general	–	in generale		in generale	–	in general
interesting	–	interessante		interessante	–	interesting
(to) like	–	piacere		piacere	–	(to) like
(to) live	–	abitare		abitare	–	(to) live
(to) love	–	amare		amare	–	(to) love
nice	–	simpatico		simpatico	–	nice
sometimes	–	qualche volta		qualche volta	–	sometimes
star	–	la stella		la stella	–	star
to	–	a		a	–	to
together	–	insieme		insieme	–	together
very	–	molto		molto	–	very
work	–	il lavoro		il lavoro	–	work

CAPITOLO 6

after	–	dopo		dopo	–	after
after that	–	dopo quello		dopo quello	–	after that
art museum	–	il museo		il museo	–	museum
bank	–	la banca		la banca	–	bank
(to) be able to	–	potere		potere	–	(to) be able to
behind	–	dietro a		dietro a	–	behind
big	–	grande		grande	–	big
bridge	–	il ponte		il ponte	–	bridge
building	–	l'edificio		l'edificio	–	building
church	–	la chiesa		la chiesa	–	church

cinema	–	il cinema	il cinema	–	cinema
closed	–	chiuso	chiuso	–	closed
correct	–	corretto	corretto	–	correct
(to) cross	–	attraversare	attraversare	–	(to) cross
department store	–	il magazzino	il magazzino	–	department store
far	–	lontano	lontano	–	far
first	–	prima	prima	–	first
floor	–	il piano	il piano	–	floor
(to) go down	–	andare	andare	–	(to) go down
(to) go shopping	–	fare la spesa	fare la spesa	–	(to) go shopping
(to) go up	–	andare	andare	–	(to) go up
grocery	–	il supermercato	il supermercato	–	grocery
immediately	–	subito	subito	–	immediately
in front of	–	avanti a	avanti a	–	in front of
left	–	sinistra	sinistra	–	left
map	–	la mappa	la mappa	–	map
minute	–	il minuto	il minuto	–	minute
near	–	vicino a	vicino a	–	near
on foot	–	a piedi	a piedi	–	on foot
open	–	aperto	aperto	–	open
park	–	il parco	il parco	–	park
post office	–	l'ufficio postale	l'ufficio postale	–	post office
pretty	–	bello	bello	–	pretty
right	–	destra	destra	–	right
(to) see	–	vedere	vedere	–	(to) see
straight	–	diritto	diritto	–	straight
street	–	la strada	la strada	–	street
(to) take	–	prendere	prendere	–	(to) take
today	–	oggi	oggi	–	today
town	–	la città	la città	–	town
(to) turn	–	girare	girare	–	(to) turn
(to) walk	–	camminare	camminare	–	(to) walk
yesterday	–	ieri	ieri	–	yesterday

CAPITOLO 7

always	–	sempre	sempre	–	always
autumn	–	l'autunno	l'autunno	–	autumn
beautiful	–	bellissimo	bellissimo	–	beautiful
brother	–	il fratello	il fratello	–	brother
different	–	diverso	diverso	–	different
during	–	mentre	mentre	–	during
especially	–	specialmente	specialmente	–	especially
everyone	–	ognuno	ognuno	–	everyone
family	–	la famiglia	la famiglia	–	family
father	–	il padre	il padre	–	father
forest	–	il bosco	il bosco	–	forest
(to) hike	–	fare alpinismo	fare alpinismo	–	(to) hike
however	–	però	però	–	however
many	–	molti	molti	–	many
month	–	il mese	il mese	–	month
mother	–	la madre	la madre	–	mother
mountain	–	la montagna	la montagna	–	mountain
often	–	spesso	spesso	–	often
(to) prefer	–	preferire	preferire	–	(to) prefer
season	–	la stagione	la stagione	–	season
sister	–	la sorella	la sorella	–	sister
(to) ski	–	sciare	sciare	–	(to) ski
spring	–	la primavera	la primavera	–	spring
(to) stay	–	stare	stare	–	(to) stay
summer	–	l'estate	l'estate	–	summer
(to) travel	–	viaggiare	viaggiare	–	(to) travel
vacation	–	la vacanza	la vacanza	–	vacation
weekend	–	il weekend	il weekend	–	weekend
which	–	quale	quale	–	which
who	–	chi	chi	–	who
winter	–	l'inverno	l'inverno	–	winter
year	–	l'anno	l'anno	–	year

CAPITOLO 8

always	–	sempre	sempre	–	always
aunt	–	la zia	la zia	–	aunt
(to) be named	–	chiamarsi	chiamarsi	–	(to) be named
sister-in-law	–	la cognata	la cognata	–	sister-in-law
family	–	la famiglia	la famiglia	–	family
hair	–	i capelli	i capelli	–	hair
hat	–	il cappello	il cappello	–	hat

husband	–	il marito	
energetic	–	energico	
in fact	–	infatti	
father	–	il padre	
father-in-law	–	il suocero	
long	–	lungo	
mother	–	la madre	
mother-in-law	–	la suocera	
(to) need	–	avere bisogno	
neice	–	la nipote	
nephew	–	il nipote	
parents	–	i genitori	
(to) play	–	giocare	
(to) put on	–	mettersi	
relatives	–	i parenti	
(to) run	–	correre	
short	–	basso/corto	
small	–	piccolo	
son-in-law	–	il genero	
uncle	–	lo zio	
wife	–	la moglie	

il marito	–	husband
energico	–	energetic
infatti	–	in fact
il padre	–	father
il suocero	–	father-in-law
lungo	–	long
la madre	–	mother
la suocera	–	mother-in-law
avere bisogno	–	(to) need
la nipote	–	neice
il nipote	–	nephew
i genitori	–	parents
giocare	–	(to) play
mettersi	–	(to) put on
i parenti	–	relatives
correre	–	(to) run
basso/corto	–	short
piccolo	–	small
il genero	–	son-in-law
lo zio	–	uncle
la moglie	–	wife

CAPITOLO 9

after	–	dopo
car	–	la macchina
cold	–	freddo
(to) come	–	venire
dear	–	caro
(to) do	–	fare
fairly	–	abbastanza
goodness	–	caspita
month	–	il mese
January	–	gennaio
February	–	febbraio
March	–	marzo
April	–	aprile
May	–	maggio
June	–	giugno
July	–	luglio
August	–	agosto
September	–	settembre
October	–	ottobre
November	–	novembre
December	–	dicembre
(to) rain	–	piovere
(to) see each other	–	vedersi
(to) snow	–	nevicare
sun	–	il sole
sunny	–	soleggiato
the next	–	il prossimo
today	–	oggi
too much	–	troppo
ugly	–	brutto
weather	–	il tempo
week	–	la settimana
(to) work	–	lavorare

dopo	–	after
la macchina	–	car
freddo	–	cold
venire	–	(to) come
caro	–	dear
fare	–	(to) do
abbastanza	–	fairly
caspita	–	goodness
il mese	–	month
gennaio	–	January
febbraio	–	February
marzo	–	March
aprile	–	April
maggio	–	May
giugno	–	June
luglio	–	July
agosto	–	August
settembre	–	September
ottobre	–	October
novembre	–	November
dicembre	–	December
piovere	–	(to) rain
vedersi	–	(to) see each other
nevicare	–	(to) snow
il sole	–	sun
soleggiato	–	sunny
il prossimo	–	the next
oggi	–	today
troppo	–	too much
brutto	–	ugly
il tempo	–	weather
la settimana	–	week
lavorare	–	(to) work

CAPITOLO 10

Afternoon	–	il pomeriggio
Anyway	–	allora
(to) ask	–	chiedere
cool	–	forte
darn	–	accidenti
drink	–	la bevanda
early	–	presto/in anticipo
evening	–	la sera
excuse me	–	scusi
half	–	mezzo
hour	–	l'ora
humor	–	l'umore
late	–	in ritardo
(to) look at	–	guardare
midnight	–	mezzanotte
minute	–	il minuto
noon	–	mezzogiorno

il pomeriggio	–	afternoon
allora	–	anyway
chiedere	–	(to) ask
forte	–	cool
accidenti	–	darn
la bevanda	–	drink
presto/in anticipo	–	early
la sera	–	evening
scusi	–	excuse me
mezzo	–	half
l'ora	–	hour
l'umore	–	humor
in ritardo	–	late
guardare	–	(to) look at
mezzanotte	–	midnight
il minuto	–	minute
mezzogiorno	–	noon

number	–	il numero	
one-way	–	andata	
platform	–	il binario	
please	–	per favore	
pleasure	–	il piacere	
remarkable	–	straordinario	
round-trip	–	andata e ritorno	
same	–	stesso	
(to) say	–	dire	
(to) think	–	pensare	
ticket	–	il biglietto	
train station	–	la stazione treni	
true	–	vero	
what	–	come/che cosa	
when	–	quando	
year	–	l'anno	

il numero	–	number	
andata	–	on-way	
il binario	–	platform	
per favore	–	please	
il piacere	–	pleasure	
straordinario	–	remarkable	
andata e ritorno	–	round-trip	
stesso	–	same	
dire	–	(to) say	
pensare	–	(to) think	
il biglietto	–	ticket	
la stazione treni	–	train station	
vero	–	true	
come/che cosa	–	what	
quando	–	when	
l'anno	–	year	

CAPITOLO 11

bathroom	–	il bagno	
behind	–	dietro	
cat	–	il gatto	
chair	–	la sedia	
comfortable	–	comodo	
computer	–	il computer	
dog	–	il cane	
downstairs	–	al piano di sotto	
during	–	durante/mentre	
exact	–	preciso	
free	–	libero	
inside	–	dentro	
lap	–	il grembo	
(to) love	–	amare	
old	–	vecchio	
outside	–	fuori	
person	–	la persona	
(to) send	–	mandare	
song	–	la canzone	
together	–	insieme	
under	–	sotto	
upstairs	–	al piano di sopra	
young	–	giovane	

il bagno	–	bathroom	
dietro	–	behind	
il gatto	–	cat	
la sedia	–	chair	
comodo	–	comfortable	
il computer	–	computer	
il cane	–	dog	
al piano di sotto	–	downstairs	
durante/mentre	–	during	
preciso	–	exact	
libero	–	free	
dentro	–	inside	
il grembo	–	lap	
amare	–	(to) love	
vecchio	–	old	
fuori	–	outside	
la persona	–	person	
mandare	–	(to) send	
la canzone	–	song	
insieme	–	together	
sotto	–	under	
al piano di sopra	–	upstairs	
giovane	–	young	

CAPITOLO 12

amusing	–	divertente	
basketball	–	la pallacanestro	
concert	–	il concerto	
enough	–	basta	
fantastic	–	fantastico	
fear	–	la paura	
friend	–	l'amico	
(to) go	–	andare	
(to) have to	–	dovere	
meeting	–	il convegno	
office	–	l'ufficio	
party	–	la festa	
(to) play an instrument		suonare	
really	–	davvero	
soccer	–	il calcio	
surprised	–	sorpreso	
(to) wait	–	aspettare	
weekend	–	il weekend	
(to) yell	–	gridare	

divertente	–	amusing	
la pallacanestro	–	basketball	
il concerto	–	concert	
basta	–	enough	
fantastico	–	fanstastic	
la paura	–	fear	
l'amico	–	friend	
andare	–	(to) go	
dovere	–	(to) have to	
il convegno	–	meeting	
l'ufficio	–	office	
la festa	–	party	
suonare	–	(to) play an instrument	
davvero	–	really	
il calcio	–	soccer	
sorpreso	–	surprised	
aspettare	–	(to) wait	
il weekend	–	weekend	
gridare	–	(to) yell	

CAPITOLO 13

appetizer	–	l'antipasto	
beef	–	il manzo	
beer	–	la birra	
bread	–	il pane	
cake	–	la torta	
cheers	–	cin cin	
chicken	–	il pollo	
fruit	–	la frutta	
ham	–	il prosciutto	

l'antipasto	–	appetizer	
il manzo	–	beef	
la birra	–	beer	
il pane	–	bread	
la torta	–	cake	
cin cin	–	cheers	
il pollo	–	chicken	
la frutta	–	fruit	
il prosciutto	–	ham	

hunger	–	la fame	
meat	–	la carne	
milk	–	il latte	
pineapple	–	l'ananas	
rice	–	il riso	
salad	–	l'insalata	
strawberry	–	la fragola	
soup	–	la zuppa	
vegetables	–	la verdura	
(to) wake up	–	svegliarsi	
wine	–	il vino	

la fame	–	hunger	
la carne	–	meat	
il latte	–	milk	
l'ananas	–	pineapple	
il riso	–	rice	
l'insalata	–	salad	
la fragola	–	strawberry	
la zuppa	–	soup	
la verdura	–	vegetables	
svegliarsi	–	(to) wake up	
il vino	–	wine	

CAPITOLO 14

arm	–	il braccio
(to) begin	–	cominciare
birthday	–	il compleanno
body	–	il corpo
busy	–	impegnato
celebrate	–	celebrare
(to) feel	–	sentirsi
foot	–	il piede
garden	–	il giardino
head	–	la testa
health	–	la salute
leg	–	la gamba
sick	–	ammalato
stomach	–	lo stomaco
tired	–	stanco
(to) wash oneself	–	lavarsi
weight	–	il peso

il braccio	–	arm
cominciare	–	(to) begin
il compleanno	–	birthday
il corpo	–	body
impegnato	–	busy
celebrare	–	celebrate
sentirsi	–	(to) feel
il piede	–	foot
il giardino	–	garden
la testa	–	head
la salute	–	health
la gamba	–	leg
ammalato	–	sick
lo stomaco	–	stomach
stanco	–	tired
lavarsi	–	(to) wash oneself
il peso	–	weight

CAPITOLO 15

better	–	meglio
business	–	il commercio
clothing	–	i vestiti
coat	–	il giubbotto
dress	–	il vestito
(to) give	–	dare
jacket	–	la giacca
(to) look for	–	cercare
pants	–	i pantaloni
ready	–	pronto
shirt	–	la camicia
size	–	la misura
shoes	–	le scarpe
socks	–	le calze
skirt	–	la gonna
that	–	quello
this	–	questo
tie	–	la cravatta
underwear	–	le mutande
(to) wear	–	mettersi
(to) worry	–	preoccuparsi

meglio	–	better
il commercio	–	business
i vestiti	–	clothing
il giubbotto	–	coat
il vestito	–	dress
dare	–	(to) give
la giacca	–	jacket
cercare	–	(to) look for
i pantaloni	–	pants
pronto	–	ready
la camicia	–	shirt
la misura	–	size
le scarpe	–	shoes
le calze	–	socks
la gonna	–	skirt
quello	–	that
questo	–	this
la cravatta	–	tie
le mutande	–	underwear
mettersi	–	(to) wear
preoccuparsi	–	(to) worry

CAPITOLO 16

(to) arrive	–	arrivare
countryside	–	la campagna
ever	–	mai
(to) find	–	trovare
fire	–	il fuoco
fortunate	–	fortunato
(to) happen	–	succedere
help	–	l'aiuto
horrible	–	orribile
life	–	la vita
(to) lose	–	perdere
now	–	adesso
police	–	la polizia
(to) receive	–	ricevere
(to) rent	–	affittare
river	–	il fiume
(to) spill	–	rovesciare
steal	–	rubare
thief	–	il ladro
tire	–	la gomma

arrivare	–	(to) arrive
la campagna	–	countryside
mai	–	ever
trovare	–	(to) find
il fuoco	–	fire
fortunato	–	fortunate
succedere	–	(to) happen
l'aiuto	–	help
orribile	–	horrible
la vita	–	life
perdere	–	(to) lose
adesso	–	now
la polizia	–	police
ricevere	–	(to) receive
affittare	–	(to) rent
il fiume	–	river
rovesciare	–	(to) spill
rubare	–	(to) steal
il ladro	–	thief
la gomma	–	tire

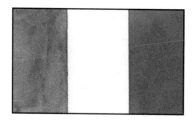

ITALY

As you embark upon your journey in Italy, be prepared to experience life as the artistic masterpiece it is. For, Italians are the masters of living. Theirs is a culture of senses, a palette of rich perspectives and an insatiable thirst for discovering the complexities of life's profound tapestry. To experience even a fraction of Italian culture will direct your mind to subtle beauties of everyday life not clearly called upon until Italy beckoned. Italy demands of her guests that the mysteries and the simple pleasures of life be experienced and comprehended. The culture will mesmerize, fascinate, provoke, and invite you to discover all things integral to living, whether considering the treasured cuisine which marks the heart of Italian life, or the complex familial relationships which weave the lifeline of Italian culture.

REGIONS

The Italian Republic combines 26 regions, from the Italian Alps of the North to the southern tip of the boot in Sicily. Each region possesses a unique identity, inherited from the millions of visitors who have settled in the territory over thousands of years.

Whereas the Milanese include origins of visitors from the northern and western European cultures, the Pugliese at the southern heel of the boot include origins from eastern European, African and Asian cultures. "When in Rome..." is a classic line used by people from all over the world which denotes this rich complexity across the variety of Italian cultures, clearly indicating the diversity of inhabitants who contribute such lovely character to the bold Italian regional cultures which make up what visitors know as "Italian."

The varied regions contribute to a population of nearly 60 million Italians across the country, embracing the fishing cultures of Venice,

Naples, and Sardinia, and the refined commercial industries of Rome, Torino, and Milan. Smaller towns such as Florence, Ravenna, and Cinque Terre each contribute an entirely different flavor of Italian culture from the larger cities of Italy. One would be missing Italian culture, were he/she not able to visit at least more than one region, for as visitors experience the varied regions, subtle and sometimes dramatic differences in the culture appear. The unique character of each region makes Italy one of the most intriguing cultures to explore.

SOCIAL CHARACTER

Italy has a long history of hosting visitors, whether invited or not. The very positioning of the elegant boot of Italy's perimeter has placed the country as a strategic focus of foreign military conquests and colonial adventurists throughout the centuries. Located in the middle of the Adriatic and Mediterranean seas, Italy provides a gateway linking east and west, north and south across the European, Asian, and African continents. It is no wonder the Italians have learned to use their national identity of social character to their advantage!

Family and friends are the very backbone of Italian culture. Without social relations, an Italian would not be "Italian." When asked who an Italian is, very likely the response will include who they are in relation to their family – they are the first son of the Rossi family from Alessandria or they are the youngest daughter of the Bonini family from Lucca.

One not only spends a lot of time daily with his/her family, but opts to be with them in good times and in bad. Italian family is the tie that binds Italians closest to their culture. The "mamma" very likely checks in with her children daily, if not every other day, to learn what has happened since they last spoke. The daily comings and goings are of most interest. To discuss one's job is only a miniscule topic for discussion when Italian family and friends gather. Last night's soccer game and a better way to cook a lasagna are of great importance to the social nature of Italian culture.

Indeed, if one is not willing to divulge morsels of personal information, as Italian culture evolves, and work responsibilities expand, Italian culture succumbs to placing one's profession at the forefront of that which is important. Yet work continues to share the limelight with family and friends, and the need to socialize, as pursuant to maintaining one's cultural identity in Italy. So long as working includes a social aspect, Italians are game.

FOOD

The art of *"mangiare"* is the heart of all things social in Italy. Regardless of the day an Italian has endured, there is always time to enjoy a pleasing meal, where the cuisine is nothing less than spectacular. In fact, Italian culture is known not only in Italy for culinary mastery, but throughout the world it is known for gastronomic perfection. The assortment of menus is limitless, from rich and creamy risottos of Lombardia to delicately sophisticated seafood linguinis of Calabria, wild boar of Tuscany to pesto gnocchi of Liguria.

Ask any Italian where the best food can be found in Italy, and they will point in two directions: (a) to their mamma's kitchen, and (b) to Emilia Romagna, a region in the heart of Italy, rightfully so. The Bolognese is famous for his/her steaming plates of spaghetti al ragu', lasagna, and hand-made tortellini. Savory dishes of prosciutto and olives decorate many a table in unassuming Emilia Romagna, where it is indeed presumed that one will feast as a king or queen.

Produce is remarkably sweet and poignant. Oranges taste like candy, broccoli as jewels of the earth. The quality of food found in markets and supermarkets alike is unparalleled in our groceries. There is an expectation of high-caliber cuisine at every table in Italy, whether at home or in a restaurant. Mealtime in Italian culture was meant for all who wish to experience cuisine as art, as mastery, as pure joy. Prepare to discuss the menu, the dish you have chosen, and the way it could always be better when you sit down to an Italian meal.

INDUSTRY

Home to many of the world's oldest and tasteful arts, Italians produce the finest of many of the world's most cherished commodities. From perfected literary works of Horace and Dante to polished Alpha Romeos and Lamborghinis, Prada and Gucci clothing and accessories to wine that is aged to perfection, Italy is a sculptress of artistic industry standards. The $1.18 trillion GDP originates from the artistic flare breathed into each and every product and service created and sold by the leading Italian industries of tourism, textiles, food processing, automobiles, furniture, and engineering. With a penchant for networking and a true love of creating art, Italian culture stages the highest standards of quality and consistency available to the world.

HIGHLIGHTS OF ITALIAN CULTURE

As you begin your journey through Italian culture, you will encounter countless treasures that will take your breath away – from the people you meet to the art you will admire, from the food and wine you will taste to the unique character of each region you will experience. Italian culture invites you to discover the variety of life, and encourages you to begin with the people who enjoy it most. Welcome to Italy, where you will learn what culture is meant to be.

Paste these removable stickers around your work and home.
It will re-enforce what you've learned!

(Ahndeeahmoh)
Andiamo.

(Nohn mee eempohrtah)
Non mi importa.

(oh fahmeh)
Ho fame.

(keh fohrtoonah)
Che fortuna!

(skoozee)
Scusi!

(ee-oh sohnoh stahnkoh)
Io sono stanco.

(vah behneh)
Va bene.

(eeoh oh sehteh)
Io ho sete.

(qooahntoh cohstah)
Quanto costa?

(ehccoh/prehgoh)
Ecco./Prego.

(cheh cohsah)
Che cosa?

(qooahleh)
Quale giorno e'?

(fahreh oonah pahssehjahtah)
fare una passegiatta

(cahpeeshee)
Capisci?

(sehcohndoh meh)
secondo me

(ahnkeeoh)
anch'io!

(ahvehreh beezohnyoh dee)
Avere bisogno di.....

(keh tehmpoh fah)
Che tempo fa?

(stah soo)
Sta' su.

(keh ohreh)
Che ore sono per favore?

(ehsehreh prehstoh)
essere presto

(ehssehreh een reetahrdoh)
essere in ritardo

(bahstah)
Basta!

(fohrteh)
Forte!

(keh kohsah fahee doorahnteh eel too-oh tehmpoh leebehroh)
Che cosa fai durante il tuo tempo libero?

(chee eh)
Ci e'...

(mahndahre oon email)
mandare un email

(stah-ee skehrtsahndoh)
stai scherzando!

(ehrah fahntahsteekohlah)
Era fantastico/a!

(keh kohsah voo-ohee mahnjahreh)
Che cosa vuoi mangiare?

(cheen cheen)
cin cin!

(boo-ohn ahppehteetoh)
Buon appetito!

(kohsah cheh)
Cosa c'e?

(sohno stahnkeeseemohlah)
Sono stanchissimo/a.

(sohnoh eempehnyahteeseemohlah)
Sono impegnatissimo/a.

(dahee)
Dai!

(nohn tee prehohkoopahreh)
Non ti preoccupare!

(eh cozee lah veetah)
E'cosi' la vita!

(keh ohrreebeeleh)
Che orribile!

(mehlyoh ahdehssoh keh mah-ee)
Meglio adesso che mai!